Skippering with confidence right from the start

THE COMPLETE
DAY SKIPPER

4TH EDITION

TOM CUNLIFFE

ADLARD COLES NAUTICAL · LONDON

Published by Adlard Coles Nautical
an imprint of Bloomsbury Publishing Plc
50 Bedford Square, London
WC1B 3DP

First edition published 2002
Reprinted 2004
Second edition published 2005
Reprinted 2008
Third edition published 2009
Fourth edition 2012

ISBN 978-1-4081-7854-6
ePDF: 9781408178560
epub: 9781408178553

A CIP catalogue record for this book is available from
the British Library.

This book is produced using paper that is made from
wood grown in managed, sustainable forests. It is
natural, renewable and recyclable. The logging and
manufacturing processes conform to the environmental
regulations of the country of origin.

Typeset in 10 on 12.5pt Sabon
Printed and bound in China by C&C Offset Printing Co

Note: while all reasonable care has been taken in
the publication of this book, the publisher takes no
responsibility for the use of the methods or products
described in the book.

CONTENTS

PREFACE

Taking charge of a yacht lifts you out of your everyday life more comprehensively than any other form of recreation. The experience can be relaxing, exciting, exhilarating, perhaps occasionally even daunting. No two trips are the same, but whatever combination a passage delivers, it will ask you to dip into the three major factors that contribute to who you are. That is why skippering is so absorbing.

Sailing inevitably involves some degree of physical activity. It may not crank up your fitness like three nights a week in the gym but, depending on the boat you choose, the process works you out as much as you want it to, and it certainly keeps you supple. Navigating safely places certain demands on the intellect, and the tactical decisions can sometimes plumb core levels of the personality; but making a passage isn't all brawn and brain. It's also about being at one with the natural world. If the wind is in the west and the tide is flooding, the combination may be useful or supremely inconvenient, but nothing you can do will alter either, until the elements roll round in their own sweet time. Accepting the ancient forces of the planet came easily to seamen in the past; it's harder for generations accustomed to centrally heated homes, the internal combustion engine and the internet, yet to do so is critical for success. It is also, to steal a phrase, the beginning of wisdom. This, coupled with the ever-changing beauty of the sea and the shoreline, furnishes the essential magical element of skippering.

This book does not set out to transform you into a Master Mariner overnight. It has been constructed to deliver a soundly based confidence in essential skills through individually achievable goals.

TOM CUNLIFFE

INTRODUCTION

When the governing body of sailing in the United Kingdom, the RYA, set up its cruising scheme under Commander Bill Anderson back in the 1970s, it accepted that if Yachtmaster Offshore were the only level of qualification on offer, many would simply shake their heads and wander off in search of a more accessible programme. Without a full time commitment extending to many months, the levels of seatime and skill theoretically demanded for Yachtmaster lie beyond the reach of someone new to the game. It was decided therefore to outline the initial steps on the ladder very carefully.

After a brief 'Introduction to Yachting' and a very basic navigation and safety course comes Competent Crew. This is a full course designed for those who want to be useful members of a cruising yacht's company. Some of the material in this book is as much to do with crewing as it is skippering, but since all skippers must master these basics, and many following the Competent Crew syllabus will choose this book to broaden their outlook, they are included in the early chapters as required information. Hot on the heels of good crewing is the primary level of taking charge.

Realising sensibly that competence in the essentials is more important than finesse, the proficiency levels recommended for skippers in their first year or two were made readily attainable. The RYA understood that while, to be safe, all the basic skills must be in place, commanding a yacht on passage after dark was one step too far. The inspired result was Day Skipper. The qualification suited not only beginners, but also more experienced sailors who were simply not interested in cruising far from home. The definition was so appropriate that it has not changed since:

'A Day Skipper is one competent to take charge of a small yacht on short daytime passages under moderate weather conditions, in waters with which he or she is familiar.'

The last item might sound like a paradox, since all must start somewhere and nobody can be familiar with the waters adjacent to their home mooring until they have arrived there in the boat. The principle is sound nonetheless, and it certainly makes sense to become familiar with one stretch of water before tackling a series of strange ones.

▶ Rocks are part of sailing and need not trouble a well-prepared skipper on the right sort of day.

A less official way of quantifying the Day Skipper is that a person who has recently achieved this standard should be capable of chartering a modest yacht on a Monday and bringing it back to base safely, and on time, the following weekend. A skipper's awareness of the limits of the qualification is therefore implicit. He'll have learned already that there's no such thing as bad luck at sea, and if it's going to blow like the clappers on Friday, this should have been foreseen. Ideally, the yacht would then be back on the mooring by Thursday evening with the skipper thinking of something useful to keep the crew out of the pubs on Friday. At worst, she will be upwind of her destination. That is good planning. So is recognising a difficult berth and choosing an easy one instead.

The successful Day Skipper soon learns that plunging in and hoping for the best is rarely as peaceful an option as hanging back and thinking things through. An old Yankee schooner skipper I sailed with used to say that the floor of the ocean is paved with optimists. I'm not sure I'd go that far because anyone who puts to sea for more than a few carefully controlled sunshine trips must have a streak of 'hope-for-the-best', but you'll take the point. Especially in the early stages while you're finding your feet, it's better to sail on the slow side with one reef more than the next boat than to career along with the side decks awash and your heart working overtime.

A practical cruising instructor has a week to bring his students up to this level of modest confidence and the success rate is high. Things were very different when I first took the helm. There were no Day Skipper courses in the 1960s. I had no mentor to keep an eye on me and put me straight, so I just climbed aboard and slipped my lines. I made a catalogue of mistakes. My early learning was painfully slow but I was very young, time was on my side and the lessons penetrated deeply.

I have never forgotten my state of mind in those days, and the misconceptions I worked with. Some of them were truly ludicrous and took years to expunge. I well recall the feeling that there was so much information in the various text books that I had sometimes forgotten the first chunk of theory before the next had made its mark. The mix of theory and practice caused major grief. So often, I found myself under pressure to shorten sail just as the water shoaled unexpectedly and I realised I was unsure of my position. It took a while to learn to prioritise.

Remembering my own experience, I have structured this guide so as to build hands-on proficiency in the order that the various areas of knowledge actually present themselves, fleshing out the theory as and when it becomes relevant. This means that, just as in real life, the lessons are not necessarily tidy packages of information following the RYA syllabus. The whole list is here because Anderson got it right, but it is packaged for someone starting from scratch on board and learning steadily, rather than as an examination guide. If you are using the book as a course companion, make full use of the index to find what you need.

Just as you, the skipper, will often be called upon to resolve which issue to tackle first, the pressing task on my own list is to get you away from the dock without delay. After an initial chapter giving you the essentials of the boat herself, you're

▶ Careful thought and preparing the crew takes the stress out of a day's yachting.

straight out on the water under power. I've decided you'd be better off coming to grips with docking and mooring procedures before you begin to take on the challenges of sailing. Most modern yachts feature a reliable diesel so powerful it can hardly be seen as an auxiliary. We'll get well on top of that from the outset, but you'll be comfortably under canvas long before you start bothering yourself with secondary port tidal calculations.

Early on, the book will give you enough pilotage basics to allow you to poke your nose outside your local harbour and stay out of trouble. There's plenty more, but if you try to grapple with the whole navigational shooting match in one chapter, your brain will be stranded at half-tide and you might sidestep the even more important business of learning to handle a boat and developing a seaman's eye.

A reasonable facility with sailing the boat is essential before you can take on even the simplest passage and, in my experience as a Yachtmaster Examiner, there is a natural tendency to cram one's head with data instead of mastering these essential skills. In any case, it's more fun to go sailing than to study waypoints, the finer nuances of meteorology and the more obscure corners of the Rule of the Road, so let's deal with such questions in their natural order, allowing each to complement the others as your competence firms up.

Within tight limits that I'll help you to recognise, it's possible to skipper a boat without knowing everything in the Day Skipper syllabus and my intention is to get you making passages you know you can cope with as soon as you can, while helping you think like a sailor. Once you're actually out there in charge, you will learn a great deal from evaluating your own experience. No book can cover all eventualities, however, and a week on the water with a good sailing school will help immeasurably. If things do go wrong occasionally, it's no good looking over your shoulder for me or your instructor to sort them out. The essence of seamanship is to accept the axiom that we are all ultimately responsible for our own mistakes.

■ Throughout the book, I've made no compromise in using seamanlike language, because many of the old terms are far more than mere jargon. They serve the vital purpose of removing ambiguity. When it has proved inconvenient to interrupt the text with a definition that many readers may not need, I have marked the first appearance of a technical word with an asterisk. You'll find its meaning in the glossary. Measurements are often given in feet and inches, simply because they sit easily with me. Much of the English-speaking world still describes boat lengths in feet and seems set to continue thus for many years to come. Although distances at sea are naturally measured in miles, not kilometres, depths are charted in metres. So are tidal heights and I have followed this division. For distances shorter than a mile, I choose yards, feet and inches. This is because a nautical mile is almost exactly 2000 yards and does not sub-divide conveniently into metres. Nevertheless, the decision is a personal one and if you hear people describing an object as '200 metres away', they are equally correct. For students locked into one persuasion or the other, a conversion table will be found in Appendix 2.

■ Boats are referred to as 'she' throughout this book. A few years back, a misguided official initiative dictated that merchant vessels should in future be called 'it'. I am delighted to advise that the Royal Navy is vigorously resisting this nasty piece of political correctness. I opt emphatically to go with the Senior Service, and I hope all thinking sailors will agree.

■ Any instructor will tell you that aspiring Day Skippers step aboard with varying degrees of knowledge. If you've already done some sailing, you'll find yourself speed-reading the first chapter or two. Don't worry about this, but do make sure you have the elementary material clear before climbing into the meatier sections. When you've worked honestly through them all, you'll have absorbed everything needed to be a complete Day Skipper. What's more, you'll understand how to make the most of your growing expertise.

ACKNOWLEDGEMENTS

This book would never have happened without my father, whose enlightened policy towards educating a difficult son involved shoving me off in a cruising boat at an alarmingly early age. I would also like to acknowledge my first shipmate and co-skipper, Martin Matthews. Heartfelt thanks are due to the following for help freely given with content and production: Keith Bessey, Andrew Bessey, David and Ellie Kendall, Ros Cunliffe, James Stevens of the RYA, Janet Murphy, the publisher, whose idea the book was, and all my Day Skipper students who have taught me more than they will ever realise.

Thanks to the Hydrographer of the Navy for permission to use extracts from British Admiralty charts, tide tables and tidal stream atlas.

Thanks to Adlard Coles Nautical for permission to use extracts from the *Reeds Nautical Almanac*.

1

WHAT'S IN A BOAT

This chapter delves into the nature and contents of the modern cruising boat. We won't deal with all her gear at this stage, because there will be plenty of opportunities to fill in the gaps. Instead, we'll begin on a 'need-to-know' basis and cover only the absolute essentials demanded by safety and your first move off the dock.

● BOARDING

Should you be used to boats, you can skip this section. If not, bear in mind two points: many accidents take place while climbing on or off a yacht, and you may be prejudged by others on the basis of how you handle yourself in this apparently obvious action.

On a marina pontoon

When the boat is moored conventionally alongside, you'll almost certainly have to clamber aboard over the guardrails*. If she's small, it may be possible to step neatly across them, but more often than not you'll have to grab something to swing yourself up and over. It's tempting and natural to use the guardrails* them- selves, but to hang your weight off these is actually a bad idea. Think it through and you'll see that because the stanchions* are supported only at their bases the leverage on the anchorage points is going to be horrific. Heave on them regularly and they will ultimately work loose and may start leaking. You'll also make the wires sag, which looks unseamanlike and lessens their effectiveness on the odd

► Try to use the shrouds to swing yourself aboard, rather than the more vulnerable guard- rails.

occasions when they must do their job. Instead, use the shrouds*. These should be strong enough to lift the boat herself and they are totally reliable. Take a firm grip, put one foot on the toerail* and pull yourself aboard.

Boarding from the dinghy

If the yacht is lying to a mooring, the best way up is to bring the tender* alongside in way of the shrouds, temporarily make fast to a stanchion*, then swing yourself aboard just as though the boat were alongside a pontoon. Unfortunately, many of today's yachts have so much freeboard* that this can't be done without a step of some sort. Often, a bathing ladder is provided at the stern*, which is convenient but not without drawbacks.

Using a stern ladder is simple enough in slack water. When there is a current running, however, it can be awkward to bring the dinghy in across the stern of the yacht. If the current is strong, come in bows-on and make sure she is secured. It'll be more awkward to hop across, but the tender is less likely to drift off leaving you doing the classic splits. If the dinghy is not an inflatable, beware of the danger of capsize.

⬤ THE HULL

The keel

Whether your boat is built of fibreglass, steel, wood, or an epoxy composite, you need to understand certain essentials about the keel. The keel serves two purposes in a sailing boat. First, it provides most of the vessel's draught* and thus lessens any tendency to be driven sideways by winds that are not from dead aft. Secondly, it carries heavy ballast to counteract the heeling effect of the wind in her sails.

The keel is sometimes moulded onto the 'canoe body' of the hull with the ballast encapsulated within it, but it is more usually attached with heavy bolts. You'll find the upper ends of these with their nuts beneath the cabin sole. Some yachts are equipped with twin keels – one each side – in order to reduce draught and enable them to take the ground upright as the tide falls.

Sea cocks

Apart from the invisible keel and the rudder, which we'll discuss shortly, what you see from a hull is more or less what you get. Leaking through the skin is rarely a problem with today's construction materials, but the integrity of the boat can be breached below the waterline in a number of places. Engines require cooling water from the sea, cockpits* and galley* sinks have drains, while heads* units demand inlet and outlet facilities. All of these, and more sometimes, have hull openings connected to their various appliances with armoured piping. The pipe is attached to the hull by means of 'skin fittings' which generally feature a valve, or sea cock. Sea cocks can be closed either by a lever or a small hand-wheel so that the boat is safe if the relevant hose or appliance fails.

A sea-cock lever is 'off' either when the wheel is tightened down – 'right is tight' – or when the lever is positioned across the piping. Shove it all the way round to rest against

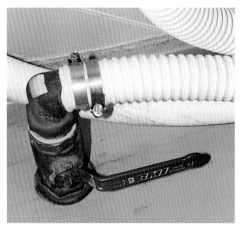 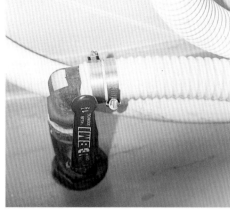

▶ A lever-style sea cock in the closed position.   ▶ The same sea cock open.

the fitting just to make sure. The cock is open with the wheel-valve unscrewed or the lever lined up with the pipe.

Nowadays, sea cocks are generally left open at sea unless protecting a device such as a sea toilet that has been found to allow water to syphon back. It's prudent to close them all when you leave the boat unattended for more than a brief run ashore.

Pumps

All yachts, even the smallest, carry at least one bilge* pump to throw the water out if it should work its way in. The regulations for small commercial craft specify two or more. These can be electrically or manually operated and, ideally, there will be more than one of each. Make certain you know where they are and how they work before leaving the dock, paying particular attention to the stowage for any removable handles. A sudden, moderate leak is nothing more than an irritation if your pumps work. If you can't find the handle, it can turn into an emergency, especially if you have been mean about buying plenty of buckets.

● THE MAST

The reality of life in most cruising yachts is that while passages may be ideally made under canvas, most manoeuvring in and out of harbour is executed under power. We won't be talking about sailing until Chapter 4, so we'll leave the attendant gear until then. The mast is so integral, however, that it needs a word up front. Whether it's wooden or an aluminium extrusion, the mast is held up by 'standing' rigging. From forward, it is supported by the forestay. From aft by the backstay. Sideways stability is provided by wires known as shrouds. The lower shrouds attach to the spar around halfway up at the quaintly named 'hounds'. The masthead shrouds are generally rigged out from the hounds by 'spreaders' to improve their angle of pull. Larger yachts might have two sets of spreaders and an intermediate set of shrouds as well. You will also see inner forestays sprouting from some masts, while others

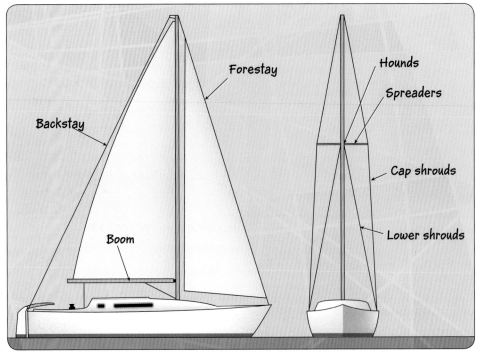

▶ Fig 1.1 Standing rigging.

sport 'baby stays' from the hounds to the foredeck, but don't worry about all this sophistication. Just remember that the stays hold the mast up fore and aft while the shrouds supply athwartships* support.

Most of the rigging wires are set up with adjustable 'bottle screws' at their lower ends. These are generally taped over to prevent chafe. Keep a regular eye on them to make sure the whole standing rig remains reasonably tight.

Note whether your mast is stepped on deck or down in the bilges. A deck-stepped mast is only as secure as its standing rigging, while its keel-stepped counterpart might get a second chance if anything fails. Emergency tow-ropes can be attached around a keel-stepped mast, but never round a spar stepped on deck.

● THE ENGINE

Most yacht engines are sited under the companionway* steps leading up from the accommodation to the cockpit. This is convenient when it comes to creating space, but a thoroughgoing nuisance when you are obliged to work on the machinery. There isn't an experienced skipper at sea without hands scarred by a spanner slipping on some inaccessible nut. Everything in a boat is a compromise, however, so when you're lying on your back cursing the designer, remember all those happy times when you didn't even notice how much room has been stolen from the engine for the crew to play in.

ENGINE CHECKS

Before starting the engine which, if inboard, is almost certainly a diesel, one or two checks must be seen to. Initially, these should be performed once every day. As you come to know a boat better, you'll find that some can be dealt with more or less frequently. There's a little more to keeping an engine happy than these initial items, but these will do to get you started.

- **Cooling** A marine engine is cooled by a water/antifreeze mix (the 'coolant') which is pumped around the cylinder block and exhaust manifold just the same as in a car, but instead of the coolant being kept down to operating temperature by a radiator and fan, it is passed through a heat exchanger cooled by circulating seawater. This is drawn into the unit by a small rotary pump, sent around the heat exchanger, then back to the sea again considerably warmed up. Final discharge may well be with the exhaust. If all is well, you will see water pulsing out of the exhaust pipe. If you don't, the cooling system is blocked. Stop the engine and check Chapter 5 to find out why.

  Before starting the engine, check the level of coolant in the plastic expansion chamber. It should be an inch or two below the cap. Top off as necessary, but never open the cap while the engine is hot. Some units do away with the heat exchanger and the coolant, being cooled instead by 'raw' seawater, in which case no check is required.

- **Sump oil** Somewhere on the engine block you will find a dipstick. Check the oil level just as you would in your motor car.

- **Stern tube** The gearbox drives the propeller by means of a shaft that passes through the hull at a waterproof 'gland'. Many glands are now of the 'deep-sea seal' type which are self-tending. The older variety involve grease-impregnated cord packing tightened down around the shaft. The gland mechanism requires regular greasing to keep the water out, and this is normally achieved by a remote grease gun. A couple of turns on the grip every few hours, and two for luck when the engine is shut down, is generally all the attention this needs. The gun is often situated in a cockpit locker or some other more or less convenient place. Keep the gun topped up with waterproof grease.

- **Gearbox** Checking the oil level in this is a 'once or twice per season' job. It's also generally awkward to gain access to the dipstick, so if the boat arrived safely in her berth and the bilge isn't polluted with oil, it's probably safe to leave it for now.

Engine controls

Some yachts, particularly power boats, have throttle and gear controls as individual levers. Most, however, use a single lever for both jobs. This has a central, neutral position in which ideally the lever is upright. A little practice enables you to 'feel' the neutral position. With the gearbox in neutral the throttle is pre-set at idling speed. A marine gearbox has only three positions: *neutral, forward* and *astern*. Move the lever gently forward and you will hear the gears engage. You'll also feel a different resistance. The engine should still be idling at the point of gear engagement. Now move the lever further forward and the engine revolutions will rise. To re-engage neutral, reduce revs to idle, then pull the lever back out of gear. Astern works identically.

When moving from ahead to astern, as you will when manoeuvring, always let the gearbox rest in neutral for a second or so on your way through. This allows the engine revs to die down, ensuring it is idling as the gear shift takes place. There is no clutch on a marine box because the water allows some degree of freewheeling for the propeller. If you crash the gears with the engine running hard you risk damaging them. Be gentle with your gearbox and, in my experience, it will last forever.

▶ A single-lever engine control, showing the neutral button in operation.

Starting and stopping the engine

■ First, make sure your batteries are ready. Most modern yachts carry at least two. If you have a dedicated engine start battery, turn it on. Some boats favour a single switch offering various combinations of domestic and engine batteries; either turn the lot on or, if one is known to be pretty flat, switch to the best.

■ You are going to need the throttle set at about half-open for a cold start. If its lever is independent, move it to the required position. Where there is a single control lever, the most common system for raising the revs without engaging gear works through a button sited below the lever. When pulled out, this disengages the gear-shift mechanism. The lever then operates the throttle only until the button is pushed in again. To operate the button, the lever must be in the neutral position. These arrangements tend to develop a mind of their own, and sometimes require a wiggle of the throttle while pulling on the button to persuade the two to work together.

■ With batteries ready, gears in neutral and throttle set, turn the key on the starter switch. Engines vary and the best advice is to follow the manufacturer's instructions, but what follows is typical:

Many engines employ a cold-start device with a warning light to indicate that it is operating. Turn the key 'one notch' to the right. You may well hear various alarms whistling. These are for temperature and oil pressure and should go off a second or two after starting. Watch the cold-start light until it goes out, then turn the key the rest of the way to activate the starter motor. Hold it on until the engine fires, release it and throttle the engine back to a fast idle while it warms up. Turn on all remaining batteries for charging if they are not already on, and check the exhaust for cooling water.

■ A diesel engine is stopped by shutting down the fuel injector pump. Until recently, this was done on a marine engine by pulling a lever. Today's engines more often shut down via the starter switch. By turning the key hard 'off' (left), a solenoid activates the pump cut-off. If your boat uses a lever, make sure after stopping the engine that it is shoved hard back to its rest position. If it is left halfway the unit will not restart.

When you have stopped the engine, turn off the engine start battery (or choose one to shut down if neither is dedicated) so you can't flatten your start potential with domestic demands.

● THE GALLEY

Some yachts are still fitted with pressurised paraffin cookers, but the vast majority of galleys are now fuelled by bottled gas. This comes in various guises, but it's essential to remember that this gas is potentially far more dangerous on board than ashore. All cooking gases are heavier than air. If unburned gas escapes in a house, it generally finds ways to dissipate itself. Aboard a boat, which is by definition water-tight, it sinks to the cabin sole and enters the bilge where, if enough is present, the air-gas mix reaches a combustible or even explosive concentration. All you need then is a spark from an electrical connection and you are facing a major disaster.

Fortunately, a sensible policy regarding galley safety virtually removes this horrid possibility. First, the gas bottle should be sited outside the accommodation, preferably in a gas-tight locker with a drain hole over the side. The bottle has a valve between it and the gas pressure regulator. Turn this off when the cooker is not in use and any gas which does manage to escape from a minute leak can be no more than the volume of the pipe itself. Make sure all piping is maintained to the highest standard by checking for leaks. Mix up a strong solution of washing-up liquid in water then lather it around any joint with a small paint brush. With the gas bottle valve 'on', you'll soon see bubbles if gas is escaping. Carefully tighten any dubious unions.

You may find a gas tap below decks close to the galley. If so, keep it shut when not cooking. More sophisticated yachts feature an electric solenoid at the gas bottle, enabling you to shut off the gas supply after every boil of the kettle by throwing a convenient switch, but the most important single safety device remains the flame failure shut-off that should be present in all cooker burners.

Unlike a domestic cooker, you don't just turn on the gas and light the flame. If you do, it will go out immediately. This is because it is protected against blowing out. The gas supply to individual burners on a quality marine cooker is automatically shut off if the temperature of the burner head falls below that of the level of ignited gas. This feature is controlled by highly reliable sensors called thermocouples which heat up quickly when the flame is burning. To over-ride them during the heat-up period, hold the control knob in for a few seconds, then release it. If the burner goes out, try again, holding the knob in for longer. Should this require more than six or seven seconds, all is not well. Clean the thermocouple sensor (a small peg standing upright close beside the burner). If that doesn't work, replace it if you can.

The final defence against escaping gas is a device called a 'sniffer'. This is a small box attached electrically to a sensor generally sited in the bilge below the cooker. If gas build-up nears a dangerous level, the sniffer sounds a loud alarm (Fig 1.2).

Make sure everyone on board understands the situation regarding cooking gas. Sort out an appropriate policy and you should enjoy a lifetime of sailing with endless hot meals, mugs of steaming tea and no danger at all.

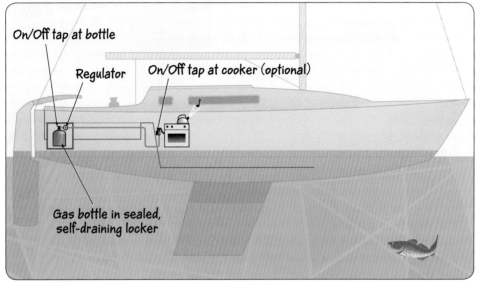

On/Off tap at bottle

Regulator   On/Off tap at cooker (optional)

Gas bottle in sealed,
self-draining locker

▶ Fig 1.2 Cooking gas safety. In addition to the basics shown, many boats also use an electronic 'gas sniffer' device in the bilge to detect any build-up. An alarm sounds if safe levels are exceeded.

SKIPPER'S TIP   FIRE EXTINGUISHERS

It's not the purpose of this chapter to deal with all the ghastly scenarios that can occur on the water, and sensible precautions backed by a bit of luck should pre-empt fire from ever breaking out on your boat. Nonetheless, it can occur at any time, so be sure you know where to find the extinguishers. More details of firefighting can be found in Chapter 15.

STEERING SYSTEMS

Rudder

All ships and boats are steered by means of a rudder. This is sited well aft. It is either hinged on the trailing edge of a long keel, or hangs vertically downwards from the hull, pivoting on its own shaft. The rudder works by interrupting the water flow under the boat to one side or the other.

Wheel

If your yacht has wheel steering, pointing her in the right direction will be one less item on the list of skills to learn. She turns just like a road vehicle, except that because the rudder is under the stern, she initiates a turn from aft rather than forward. In this respect, steering a boat going ahead is similar to guiding a car that's reversing. There, you're considering what's happening to the front wings as the wheels swing them round. With a boat, you're obliged to watch your quarters* when making a tight turn close to an obstacle (see Chapter 2). Steering when the boat is going astern, stand looking aft and turn the wheel the way the boat is to go (Fig 1.3).

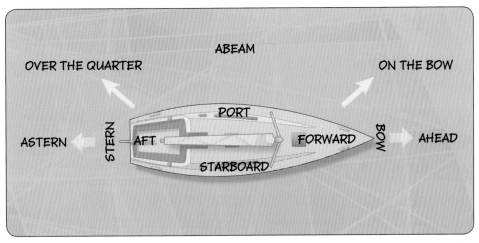

▶ Fig 1.3 Some basic sailing terms. Using the traditional terminology of the sea promotes a seamanlike attitude. Start off correctly and in no time these and other terms will sound totally natural. They have the benefit of complete lack of ambiguity.

Tiller

A tiller has much to recommend it on a boat under 35ft or so. It's quick, direct, reliable, simple and cheap. Unfortunately, it can confuse the beginner. I remember one of my friends shoving a tiller the wrong way in a river and, as the boat began to drift towards the mud, he panicked and pushed harder and harder. We ran aground comprehensively and had plenty of leisure to work out what went wrong.

The answer is always to take your time until you're thoroughly used to the tiller. Think of it as a continuation of the rudder blade extending forward of the rudder's bearings. If you are going ahead and you want to turn to starboard*, the rudder blade must be held in that direction, so move the tiller to port*. Going astern, face aft and imagine the rudder leading the boat the way you want her to swing. If this is to port, heave the tiller to starboard. Just one warning: a tiller can get mighty heavy when the boat's going astern, so be ready to show it who's boss.

2

MOVING THE BOAT

Most passages start and end with the engine. If the essential manoeuvring skills are in hand from the outset, one of life's major worries is under control. To put things in perspective, there isn't a professional skipper in the Mediterranean who doesn't breathe a secret sigh of relief when his yacht slides sweetly into a tight berth between two expensive classics and the stern lines snake ashore. He makes it look easy, but that's only because his crew know exactly what is expected of them and he is obeying the same set of rules that we're going to look into now. Berthing or leaving a berth in a modest yacht isn't difficult, but you can make it a great deal easier if you understand what is going on.

● THEORY

Pivoting

When we were discussing steering systems in the previous chapter, we noted that a boat swings her stern out when the rudder is put over. The full story is that she actually swivels, or pivots about a theoretical point somewhere in the keel. If you steer hard to port when the boat is going ahead, the rudder moves to that side, the stern swivels away from it to starboard, and because the boat is rigid, her head pivots the other way. The rest of her follows the bow and she turns to port.

The first result of this critical feature of all boats is that if you are lying alongside a berth you can't simply 'drive out' as you can in a car. If you try, the stern will bang into the pontoon and the bow will be unable to swivel outwards. It is therefore important to shove the bow off, or find some other way of persuading it to point the way you want to go.

The same rule about the swinging stern applies when you are manoeuvring amongst other boats, or obstacles in general. It's common to miss this vital detail. Burn it into your soul and you'll save the price of this book ten times over in bills for scraped topsides* (Fig 2.1).

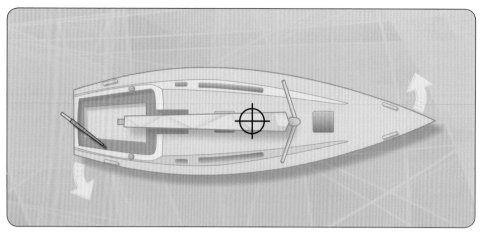

▶ Fig 2.1 Essential manoeuvring. Rather than turning from the bow like a car, a boat swivels around her keel. Steering to port like this, the stern pivots to starboard, swinging the bow round to port as it does so. Understanding this principle is vital in close manoeuvres.

Prop-wash

Because your propeller is spinning round, it creates a sideways force as well as its drive forward or astern. Barely noticeable when the boat is moving ahead at cruising speed, this effect cannot be ignored when the propeller is turning astern. On some boats, particularly those with long keels, the propeller sluices its wash so hard to one side that it literally walks the stern of the boat round, regardless of what the rudder is doing. There are various terms for this, but I favour the self-explanatory 'prop-walk'.

Whenever you go astern there will be some tendency to prop-walk. Depending on the boat, this might be substantial or minimal. It can work for you or against you but, with preplanning, it can often be turned to advantage. If the stern on your boat slides to port, 'port-side to' docking will be preferred if no other factors are involved. Should you try to come in 'starboard-side to', you'll probably manage, but when you put the engine into astern to take off way, instead of neatly tucking herself into the berth, the boat will throw her quarter away from it, leading to an untidy scramble ashore with the lines. If some other factor has dictated that you must come in 'against the prop', apply as little astern power as possible, or be prepared for a messy result (Fig 2.2).

Determining prop-walk

Make sure the boat is secure against the pontoon, or firmly moored to her buoy. Run the engine at slow revs astern and look over both quarters. The chances are that much more wash will be appearing on one side than the other. If the boat were floating freely, she would tend to prop-walk her stern away from this wash, so that is your answer. Just for the record, if she shoves her stern to port in reverse, the propeller is rotating clockwise when driving ahead and is thus 'right-handed'. A 'left-hander' generates the opposite effect.

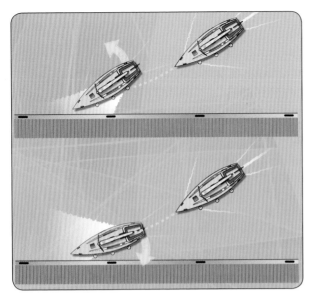

▶ Fig 2.2 Docking under power. Above: there is a tendency in some modern yachts to throw the stern to starboard when the engine is run astern. Such craft are uncomfortable docking 'port side to' where there are currents running. Below: this yacht's propeller washes her stern in to port when running astern. 'Port side to' docking is therefore the favoured option where wind or tide do not dictate otherwise.

Cross-winds

The effect of a cross-wind on a yacht varies inversely with the speed she is making. Moving steadily, her keel works efficiently. As she loses way it becomes less effective until, just before she stops altogether, it stalls and the boat's head 'blows off' to leeward*. At the same time, because little or no water is flowing past the rudder, this too ceases to function and the skipper becomes the victim of the breeze. If you are ready for it, a cross-wind can be observed before it becomes a nuisance and, like prop-walk, it can be neutralised or even made to work in your favour by setting up the manoeuvre with the effect in mind.

Combined effects

Prop-walk and cross-winds both make the boat swing her bow predictably at low speeds. With each working in the same direction, the combined outcome can sometimes make a boat uncontrollable. A boat whose stern naturally prop-walks to port, as she starts to go astern, will receive a doubly hard time from a strong wind on her port bow. The wind blows her head off to starboard and hence, through her willingness to pivot, the stern's tendency to swing to port is magnified. The result may be that the bow slides away to starboard beyond your power to correct it.

There is only one answer to this. You must assess the conditions and if this seems a likely development, don't try the manoeuvre. On the other hand, a cross-wind can sometimes be harnessed to counteract prop-walk, enabling the boat to move away sweetly astern, steering almost from the start.

Upwind or downwind?

Left to themselves, all sailing boats and some power-driven craft take up a position with the quarter to the wind. Motoring astern upwind, a yacht is therefore in her natural state, leaving her rudder with only modest amounts of work to do. Motoring astern downwind, on the other hand, can be a nightmare. The bow will try to blow off, perhaps exacerbated by prop-walk, so much so that until the boat has built up considerable way, the rudder cannot counteract the forces of darkness.

Some boats simply slide off, beam to the wind, and refuse to steer at all, leaving skippers complaining about 'unpredictable handling' and a boat 'with a mind of her own'. If you must work into or out of a berth astern, bear these factors in mind when planning your tactics. Forewarned is forearmed, and so long as you are aware of what may happen, none of them need create insoluble problems.

● DEALING WITH SHORE LINES

If a boat of anything over 20 feet or so is to be kept neatly alongside her berth, she needs more than just a bow line and a stern line. In a flat calm these might work well enough on their own, but as soon as the good old cross-wind comes along, the bow blows in or out and the answer is to rig spring lines as well (see overleaf).

Spring lines, or 'springs' as they are generally known, run forward from the stern and aft from the bow. The bow spring originates from the bow, and vice-versa. Because they run more nearly parallel to the boat's fore-and-aft axis than the bow or stern lines, the springs stop the boat surging forward or backward, allowing the bow line and stern line to do their jobs of keeping her close to the dock.

Springs can also be used to help a boat off a dock when she is being blown on. If you remove all the lines except the stern spring then motor astern against it, the bow will swing out, often more effectively than you can hope to manage merely by shoving. Even better results are sometimes achieved by motoring ahead against a bow spring to force the stern off the wall. This work is particularly effective if

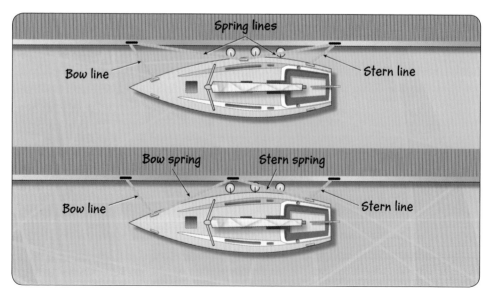

▶ Fig 2.3 Dock lines. Above: the marina moor. Securing alongside using an amidships cleat or fairlead* for the 'springs' is sometimes convenient in the controlled world of the yacht marina. Below: the classic moor. Strictly speaking, springs should originate from bow and quarter. This enables them to fulfil all their potential functions.

you use the rudder to 'steer' into the dock because it diverts the gush of water from the propeller sideways, literally sluicing the stern away from the pontoon, and helping the spring line in its work (Fig 2.3).

Making fast

Before leaving your berth for the first time, you must be reasonably familiar with basic line practice. Some instructors demand particular ways of making fast, but time has taught me to steer clear of dogma. The truth is that a number of different methods work equally well. There is only one general standard for me: however you make a rope up, it must stay secure until the time comes to let it off. It must then be capable of being eased and released, whatever the load. Here are some pointers towards achieving this end:

■ You have four lines controlling your boat. Each should be an individual rope. Don't try to make one or two do the whole job, or you'll end up with a cat's cradle where one line cannot be adjusted without letting another off. This is often the last thing you want, so insist on the good habit of 'one rope, one job'. You'll see experienced people securing in marinas by taking a long line, making off the bitter end* on the bow, carrying the rest ashore, cleating* off the bight* on the dock, then 'bringing the end back for a spring'. This works most of the time and can make things initially simpler for short-handed crews, but it's untidy and one day will end in tears when the boat is against an old-fashioned wall with a big tidal fall rather than a neat, clean marina pontoon. For what it's worth, my wife and I use four ropes for our 40-footer even if there's just the two of us and the berth is dead simple. We've found that in the long run it saves trouble.

■ Try to put only one rope on an individual cleat or bollard. If you double up, you can be sure that the rope you'll want to ease in a gale the following day will be the bottom one.

■ Secure the bitter end of the mooring line ashore so that you can make adjustments from on board. It's more seamanlike, no passer-by will trip over your coil and no vandal can chop himself off a quick few fathoms* of your finest three-strand.

■ Probably the favourite way to secure a line ashore is with a non-slip loop called a bowline (see photos on p16). This has the advantage of being quick to tie, unwilling to come undone under load, yet always 'breakable' when you are ready to untie it. A loop can be rapidly dropped over a cleat or a mooring post. If you are obliged to make fast to a ring, tie the bowline into it with an extra turn to minimise chafe. Given a cleat ashore, you might prefer to take a few figures-of-eight. I have no quarrel with this. It just takes a little longer.

Using a bowline to secure a shore line is sometimes criticised by the uninitiated on the grounds that it cannot be untied under load. This is no problem at all if you have made the line fast on board the boat in a seamanlike manner. Some people are always uneasy about the danger of the loop slipping off a cleat, although I have not found this a problem. If in doubt, make a larger loop and pass it around twice.

▶ The bowline is perhaps the most important single knot you will use on board.

■ To cleat a line, whether it be a mooring or a piece of running rigging, remember the golden rule. It must stay fast until needed, then come away without fuss. A successful way of achieving this is to take the rope once around the cleat, then lay on a couple of 'figures of eight' before finishing with a further round turn. If the cleat is big enough to make this appropriate, you have a set-up that will hold an ocean liner.

Where the cleat is on the small size for the rope, try missing out one or other of the round turns then finishing with a locking hitch instead. This is done by 'turning over' the final half of the last figure of eight and pulling it tight so that it locks on itself. If you don't use two full figures of eight in front of it, there is some danger of the locking hitch tightening on itself and being awkward to let off. Use a locking hitch with caution, therefore, but never feel ashamed of doing so.

Coiling and stowing

Once away from the berth, all shorelines should be stowed, ideally in a cockpit locker where they will be handy. Take the rope in your left hand with the palm towards you. Now coil into this hand using your right, making loops about 18 inches across. It is important that the rope is coiled clockwise. This may not matter in the case of braidline, but three-strand rope has an in-built memory and will kink if coiled backwards, or 'against the lay'. Get into the habit from the outset of always coiling any rope 'with the sun', regardless of its type, and you'll never make a mistake with one that matters.

▶ There are several ways of making fast to a cleat, but this one is generally approved and easy to apply. 'A round turn, one or two figures-of-eight, and a second round turn to finish off'. When securing to a cleat (a–d), where space is limited for turns, it is perfectly acceptable to use a locking hitch (e–f).

The best way of 'making up' a line for stowing is sometimes called the 'gasket coil hitch'. Wrap several turns round the middle of the coil, catching the first one in, then pass a bight through between them and the end of the coil. Now hand the loop over the top of the coil and snug it down tight (see photos overleaf).

Rope types

Dock lines are usually selected on size and price. Ideally they will be polyester, which has low stretch characteristics combined with strength and chafe resistance, and is also reasonably resistant to attack by UV light. Polyester used for halyards

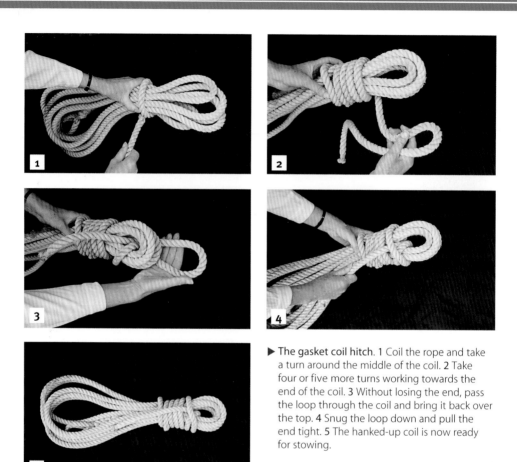

▶ The gasket coil hitch. 1 Coil the rope and take a turn around the middle of the coil. 2 Take four or five more turns working towards the end of the coil. 3 Without losing the end, pass the loop through the coil and bring it back over the top. 4 Snug the loop down and pull the end tight. 5 The hanked-up coil is now ready for stowing.

needs to have the lowest stretch characteristics available, so it is usually bought in its 'pre-stretched' variety.

A popular alternative to polyester is the spikier polypropylene that has the advantage of being light enough to float. It chafes more easily, however, and after a few years is rendered unserviceable by sunlight. It makes tolerable shorelines or heaving (throwing) lines, but it leaves much to be desired when it comes to running rigging.

The third common rope variant is nylon, favoured specifically for anchor lines because of its enormous strength and elasticity. It stretches to a considerable proportion of its own length before breaking – a desirable characteristic for anchor ropes or towing (where the stretch absorbs shock) but not what you want in your running rigging.

Higher-tech ropes such as Dyneema or Spectra are sometimes found in halyards where low stretch characteristics are vital. These modern variants extend under load as little as wire and are, of course, far lighter. The casual observer might mistake some forms for polyester, but they are a very different animal. Often in lurid colours, other forms can look perfectly ordinary, but they are all wolves in sheep's clothing.

● LEAVING THE BERTH

Lifejackets

Before getting under way, you'll have to make a decision about whether to wear life jackets. Time was when these were cumbersome, their very awkwardness half-negating any safety factors they might convey for every-day wear. Today's self-inflating 'lifer-plus-harness' kits are unobtrusive and comfortable. If funds run to these, they are as easy to slip into as a waistcoat. On the other hand, many experienced sailors rarely wear lifejackets because they can swim and, in fair weather, a yacht is a pretty safe place to be. You are responsible for yourself and your crew, but thank goodness that, in private seafaring at least, realism still comes before political correctness. The answer is therefore a personal one. Do whatever you feel comfortable with.

The swinging mooring

If you are secured to a swinging mooring, leaving is easy. Start the engine, slip the mooring line, wait for a second or two for the boat to drift back from it, then motor away. If tide or wind are driving the boat up over the mooring buoy, put the engine astern and gently back away, always bearing in mind that you must not, under any circumstances, allow the mooring or any other rope to come near your propeller. Everyone seems doomed to foul their propeller at least once just for the experience, but you won't want to do it a second time, and you certainly don't want to start right now.

Alongside berths – the question of current

Before leaving an alongside berth it is vital to assess any tidal stream. If the boat is not moving 'over the ground' but the water is, she is effectively making way relative to the water. With her head up to the stream, the rudder will bite immediately and you have full control right from the outset. If the boat is lying stern to the current, she is strictly making sternway. If you try to move out of the berth by going ahead, you will have no control at all until you have 'caught up' with the current and overtaken it. Only then can water flow over the rudder blade in the direction you want. You will be drifting downstream all the time this process is going on, and may well have hit something before you gain control two or three boat's lengths down tide. The only way to ensure full command from the outset is to move off against the current. If this means leaving stern first or even using ropes to turn around, then so be it.

Assessing the current

I once sat in the cockpit of a yacht during her skipper's Yachtmaster examination. He was deciding whether to leave the berth by going ahead or astern when, to my astonishment, he asked his mate to pass up the tide tables.

'What do you want those for?' I asked.
'To see which way the tide's flowing,' was the prompt response.

We were in fact near the turn of tide in an area notorious for strong streams. He forgot to add an hour for 'summer time' to the posted data and got it wrong. We pranged the boat ahead and the candidate failed. All he need have done was use his eyes to look at the water beside the boat. If you can't see any minibow waves on posts, buoys or moored craft, and are in genuine doubt, spit discreetly over the side and watch the bubbles.

The sea is often like that. Things can be so much simpler than they seem.

● PRACTICAL BOAT HANDLING

Taken all that theory on board? Right. Check the weather. If it's blowing hard, go to the pub. If not, it's ensign* up and... let's do it!

If this is the first time you have ever moved a boat, you must be extremely wary of the effects of the tide, not only when leaving and returning to the berth, but also when under way in confined waters. If you have any doubts about your berth being tricky, wait for slack water* in the first instance and always steer well clear of obstructions lest an unexpected current set you onto them. If the tide can run strongly past your berth and there is a possibility that it might be behind you when you return, make sure that this does not happen by timing your arrival for slack water, or at least so that you will be heading up into a gentle stream. If in doubt about how to do this, check Chapter 3.

If you are likely to be beset by other boats, check the early part of Chapter 3 to find out about the Rule of the Road.

Leaving an alongside berth

Classically, a boat lies alongside a berth with all her options open and the tide running along it one way or the other. This is the situation we will consider. Yours may be more complicated, especially if you are on an inside marina berth, but one can only start at the beginning. The lessons of the perfect scenario will stand you in good stead regardless of where you are ultimately berthed.

SKIPPER'S TIP   USE OF SLIP ROPES...

If your crew are uneasy about hopping aboard as the boat leaves the dock, or if the wind is blowing you off so that there is a possibility of unwittingly leaving them behind, it pays to opt for 'slip ropes' so that the dynamic part of the process can be managed from on board. To rig a slip, take the line in question off the shore cleat, pull through some slack, pass the bight round the cleat and send the end back to the boat. Both ends are now aboard. When you are ready, you've only to let go the shorter end and pull the line in from around the shore cleat.

If the original line is loaded up heavily, use a spare line to rig the slip. Once the slip rope is tensioned, ease away the old single line, bring it aboard, and you're ready to go.

Slipping ropes in this way occasionally fouls up. Rigging them is time-consuming and hard on middle-aged backs. Therefore, only deploy them when you really need them. Typically, you might rig slips on bow line and stern spring when leaving a tricky berth with the tide running towards you. Perhaps with a strong wind blowing you off, you would drop the springs and rig slips on bow and stern lines. It is almost never necessary to rig more than two. Often one will do, and on many occasions none is needed. To rig them regardless is pedantic and an annoyance to the troops.

■ **No tide** Have your crew take in the springs first, followed by bow and stern lines, shove the bow off then hop aboard as you engage gear and cruise slowly out of the berth.

■ **Tidal stream from ahead** You can tackle this very neatly by taking in the bow spring first. Give it a wiggle before you do. It's probably not loaded at all. Next move a fender to a point well aft on the quarter and take in the stern line followed by the bow line. The boat will now swing out against her stern spring, rolling around the fender. Help her with a touch astern on the engine if need be. Once you are pointing as you wish, the crewman lets off the spring and steps aboard. As you go ahead, the stream will set you away from the dock with a touch of sideways drift. Very elegant.

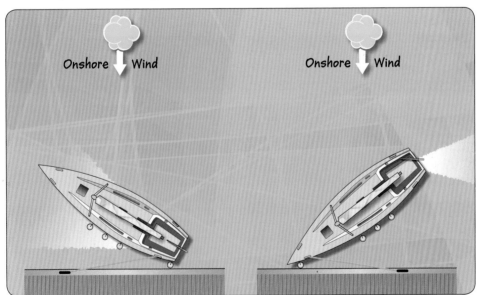

▶ Fig 2.4 Springing off. Left: motoring astern against a stern spring forces the bow off the dock. The rudder position is irrelevant because the stern is immobile. Right: to spring the stern off the dock, motor ahead against the bow spring, using the rudder to direct the prop-wash. Note the use of the fender in both situations.

If you feel this is all too complicated, just throw off the springs followed by the stern line. The head will now swing in untidily, but never mind. Steer away from the dock, and, as your crew brings in the bow line and shoves off, put her slow ahead and off you go. It's important that the bow line is the last off in this case. If this had been the stern line, there would be nothing to stop the boat drifting astern until it brings her up short. She would then swing her bow messily out into the stream with consequences that might be far from ideal.

■ **Tidal stream from astern** This time you'll leave by going astern, so it's stern spring off first, then bow line. You are now tethered by bow spring and stern line. As soon as you let off the stern line, the stern will swing out, so place a fender a little abaft* the bow in good time. You can now release the spring to go astern into open water. If you don't have enough crew, just throw off everything except the stern line, then bring that in as you engage gear (Fig 2.4).

Fenders

These are hung from the guardrails by their lanyards*. It's important to attach them near to stanchions. If you don't, their weight will create saggy wires which, as we have already noted, look unseamanlike. For this reason, some skippers insist on making the lanyards off somewhere other than the guardrails. I can understand this, and if you can find somewhere better that does not trip people up, go for it.

Fenders are best attached using a clove hitch backed up by a single half hitch (see photo below). They are the first thing taken in when you leave a berth and the last thing deployed just before you return. Never, ever, sail around with them hanging over the side.

▶The clove hitch is quick and easy to tie, once you have acquired the knack. It has a number of applications, perhaps the most common being to hitch a fender lanyard to a guardrail. If used for this, a half hitch clapped onto the part between the knot and the fender gives added security.

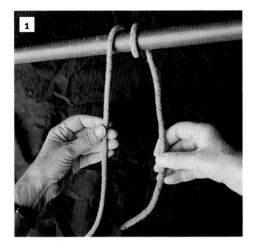

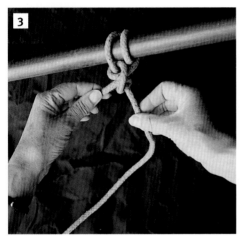

▶The round and two half hitches. This knot is extremely easy to tie and can be used whenever a rope is to be secured to a static object. It works for fenders as an alternative to the clove hitch, for dinghy painters, bucket lanyards, etc.

1 The round turn is what really carries the load. The half hitches merely hold it in place. Make sure you pass the rope round all the way as shown, not just halfway. **2/3** Make the half hitches as shown and they won't lock up.

Free-floating exercises

It's sad but true that most sailors never really discover the subtleties of their boats' behaviour. They just manage as best they can, learning in a haphazard sort of way as they go along. To be on top of the job from the start, you must set aside an hour or two to experiment. Find a quiet spot somewhere near the berth with a bit of sea room and deep water. Take the engine out of gear and let the boat drift to a standstill. Now try the following:

■ **Steering astern** Consider prop-walk and cross-winds, then take her away. Just watch out for the tiller if you have one. Once a yacht is making walking pace astern, this can do you a serious mischief if you let it get too far across. As soon as she's moving well, small movements and a firm grip are the order of the day.

Next, try her with the wind on different bows. Motor upwind then downwind and feel the difference. Find out how fast you have to go to overcome the prop-walk. See if a cross-wind can help. Get to know what she'll do and what she won't.

■ **The short turn** You'll have worked out which way the stern kicks before leaving the dock. Now practise using it to turn in the shortest possible distance. Stop the boat and, if her prop is going to throw the stern to port, steer hard to starboard. Give the engine a four or five-second burst ahead so that the propwash slams into the rudder, throwing the stern round. As soon as she starts to gather way, put her into neutral, then run her half astern until all way is off. Watch her pull herself into the turn with the propeller. Unless you actually gather more than a knot of stern way there's no point in moving the helm from where it is. It won't be working anyway. Now go ahead again, and so on until the yacht has turned through 180°. Next, try the same manoeuvre 'against the prop' and see if she performs differently. Notice whether the variation is slight or pronounced, one day you'll need to know (Fig 2.5).

■ **Keel stall** Steer at moderate speed so as to put the wind abeam. Now take her out of gear and let her lose way. At some stage before she stops altogether, the bow will start to blow away and you'll need more and more helm to keep her going straight. The keel is now stalling. See how much throttle you need to recover control. Now find out how big a burst produces the same effect. This sort of 'feel' for a boat is most useful when coming alongside or picking up an object or a casualty from the water.

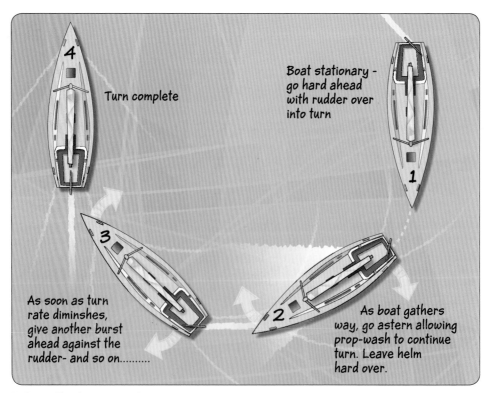

Boat stationary - go hard ahead with rudder over into turn

Turn complete

As soon as turn rate diminshes, give another burst ahead against the rudder- and so on..........

As boat gathers way, go astern allowing prop-wash to continue turn. Leave helm hard over.

▶ Fig 2.5 The short turn under power.

● RETURNING TO THE BERTH

When you are satisfied you have learned something of how your boat behaves under power, head back to your berth and read the next chapter before venturing further afield. If you are on a mooring, head up to it from down-tide so that you lose way as your crew picks up the buoy with the boathook. If there is no tide, approach from down-wind.

Where your berth is alongside, approach from down-tide, 'head-up' to the stream, with your lines ready. Fenders should be hitched on in good time and slung over the rail just before you arrive. If you're short-handed, it pays to make fast the bight of bow and stern lines on board, then have your crew carry as much as they think they'll need, plus half that again for contingencies. Come in as slowly as you can, ideally at an angle of about 30°, taking care always to retain steerage way. If there's a strong tide, you'll be drifting sideways, so line up some feature of your berth (a plank, maybe, or an electricity or hose fitting) with something in the background and steer so as to keep them 'on'. The fact that you and the two objects

are remaining in line means that you are sliding into your berth on a straight path and are not being shoved away by the stream. When the current is strong enough and the berth is tight, you can almost slide sideways into it at a right angle by using this method of observation and keeping your speed down. The concept, known as 'working a transit', is extremely important in tidal waters and pervades almost all you do. It's vital in navigation and pilotage as well as boat handling.

If you're still moving ahead when you arrive alongside, take off the last of your way with a steady burst astern as you straighten up, remembering any possible prop-walk effects. Now have your team step ashore from the vicinity of the shrouds with bow and stern lines. They should make these up temporarily on cleats just forward and astern of the boat so as to keep her more or less parallel to the dock. Once things are stable, make the ends fast and take up the slack on board. Now run out the springs, treat yourself to a nice mug of tea and take time to sift the lessons of your findings.

Two last jobs: Drop your ensign as the sun sets and consult Appendix 1 (checklist for leaving the boat) before you go home.

3

FIRST VENTURES

Having made your initial moves off the berth, the next logical step is to leave harbour, take a look at the sea-world outside, relate it to the chart and return safely. You may feel you want to set out on a passage straight away, and I can understand that, especially if you have some sea time under your belt. If you're a beginner, however, you aren't ready for that yet. You need to work through a few more chapters first. In any case, there are a number of core skills that cannot be side-stepped. These are set out here, structured so as to augment your hands-on learning experience.

If you haven't a suitable vessel handy and are taking a shore-based theory course, you'll find the basis of chartwork and pilotage in this chapter, as well as the essentials of the quaintly named Rule of the Road. The rest of the navigation syllabus is plumbed in through subsequent chapters at the stages it will be required to complement your growing confidence as a skipper. We aren't going to hoist any sails at this stage, but if you can sail already, by all means take a short cruise around when you're in open water.

● READING THE CHART

Keeping a yacht on track close to the coast involves pilotage more often than full-on navigation. Pilotage can be defined as eyeball chartwork rather than plotting with pencil and rulers. The latter, or its electronic equivalent, comes into its own further offshore. It certainly has a place on the shorter trip, but it's a mistake to imagine that as soon as you leave harbour you are expected to be down below working out tidal vectors and three-point fixes. Pilotage has its own skills which are called for at the beginning and end of every passage, so we'll start with its basics.

You can't go anywhere without knowing if there is enough water to float you all the way. The paper chart or an electronic plotter supplies all the information required for this in two-dimensional form. Various types of chart are available, as are diverse plotter displays if you opt for the silver screen. Even if you see a bright future with the electronic plotter, however, you must always maintain a traditional backup. An old-fashioned chart also provides a superior overview so, for the moment, we're going to stick with paper charts. For this book, I've preferred those produced by the Admiralty.

They aren't always the cheapest, but they are certainly the clearest, and the chart table-sized Small Craft Folios of different coastal zones are extremely useful.

Orientation

Select a large-scale (zoomed-in) chart showing your harbour entrance and the surrounding waters. You'll be aware of what you can see outside the harbour. If the chart doesn't encompass the complete picture, have a smaller scale one standing by. Note that the vast majority of charts are in 'north-up' format. This means North is at the top. If at any stage you become disorientated, glance at your compass, note where north is and relate this to the chart, 'right way up'.

Scale

You'll notice a scale running up both sides of the chart. There is a different one at top and bottom, but don't concern yourself with this yet. The one at the sides represents latitude which is stated in degrees (0 – 90 north or south of the equator). Each degree divides into 60 minutes which subdivide into ten decimal points known as 'cables', after the span of a single length of a Nelsonian warship's anchor rope. It so happens that a minute of latitude equals one nautical mile. A mile at sea is around 2000 yards, so a cable is 200 yards. Don't get tied up with metres here. Distance measurements at sea predate the EU, and metric madness doesn't work. Only depths have succumbed. Kilometres have nothing to do with speed at sea either – this is measured in nautical miles per hour, or 'knots'.

Study your chart, actively relate the scale to what you can see, and if you have a speed log, use it to familiarise yourself with what a knot feels like in terms of walking pace, a jog-trot, etc (Fig 3.1).

Direction

This will be considered in detail in the later chapters on navigation. For now, we can take it that if you are physically facing north, you are looking towards the top of the chart. South is dead behind you, west to your left and east to the right.

Depths

All over the chart you will see numbers in italic script. These represent soundings, or the depth of the water at that spot measured in metres. The main number is the depth and any subscript is a decimal. Thus 9_6 represents a depth of 9.6 metres. You may still find a venerable old chart where depths are given in fathoms and feet so, just to make absolutely sure, check in the top margin where you will find the units plainly stated. You may also see soundings on green areas with a line under them, thus: $\underline{0}_3$. These refer to areas which are 'dry' at Low Water, but which may be covered by a rising tide.

All charted depths are referred to 'Chart Datum' (CD). This is the water level at 'Lowest Astronomical Tide' (LAT), a theoretical minimum which is the lowest tide normally predicted by Admiralty tide tables. The tables work their data from the positions of sun and moon whose gravitational pulls control the tide. Hence the name,

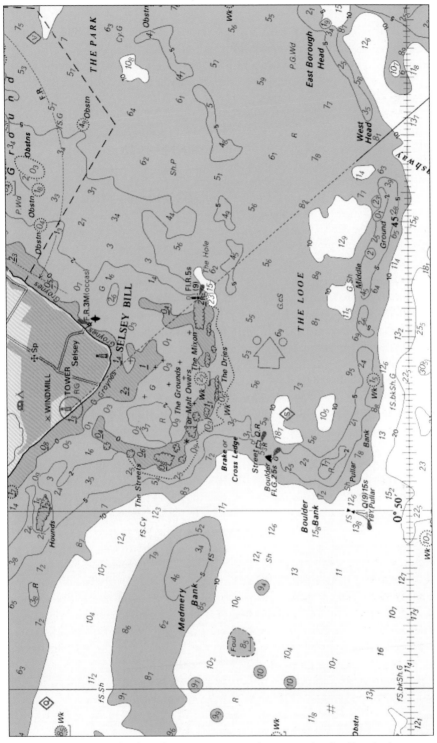

▶ Fig 3.1 British Admiralty chart showing contours, and an inserted scale of longitude.

'astronomical'. It is obscurely possible for a tide to fall lower than this, but only when it is affected by extraneous meteorological influences. Regardless of the state of tide, therefore, if you operate from a fall-back position that except on the rarest of occasions there will never be less water than the chart says, you're unlikely to be disappointed.

Contours

The depths on any chart are organised around contour lines. Depending on the scale of the chart, these might be set at 0, 2, 5, 10, 15 and 20 metres. Their presence makes reading a chart much easier. The 0m (zero metre) line is found between the dark blue-coloured water and the green drying areas – literally at the water's edge at LAT. At the 2m contour, the blue pales out a notch, and outside the 5m line the water becomes white.

The depth sounder

One of the most important navigation tools on board is the echo sounder. Virtually all yachts now have one of these. If yours hasn't, you must equip yourself immediately with a leadline and develop proficiency at using it. Come to think of it, even if you do have a sounder, go out and buy a lead, tie it onto 20m or so of light braidline and stow it somewhere handy as an inexpensive back-up.

Even if you lack navigational sophistication you can stay out of trouble so long as you can read the chart like a road map, don't allow yourself to become disorientated and keep an eye on the echo sounder to make sure things add up. Bear in mind, however, that if the water is comparatively shallow and the tide forms a significant factor in its depth, for most of the time your reading is not going to be the same as the charted sounding. See the section below on tide tables to make a sensible correction, and always bear in mind that if you are cutting things fine, the depth of the sounder's transducer unit below the surface may become important.

Transducer depth

All echo sounders measure the distance between the transducer and the sea bottom. The transducer is generally sited low on the boat's canoe body (not in the keel), so it could be anything from 0.3m to 1m or so below the surface. The first thing to ascertain is what this distance is. Ideally, you should measure it when the boat is dried out and, while you are at it, run the tape over her draught as well, measuring from the scum line where she actually floats. If she is freshly painted, take a line three inches or so below the upper end of the boot top* for a typical 25-footer. Where a boat is afloat, you'll have to rely on the builder's spec for draught and, unless he can tell you, take a guess at transducer depth.

An uncalibrated echo sounder can only read what is below its transducer, so you must add its depth to all readings to ascertain the actual depth of water.

SKIPPER'S TIP — CALIBRATING AN ECHO SOUNDER

Some sounders can be calibrated, allowing them to read any depth you like. The two most popular results of calibration are to read 'actual depth of water' and 'depth below the keel'. I have my own set to 'depth of water', because I know full well what my draught is, so if the instrument reads that, I'm aground. It's easier to relate depths to the chart when the sounder states the real depth of the water.

Alternatively, if your sounder cannot be calibrated or you don't want to bother with such technicalities at this stage, just add 'transducer depth' in your head to all its readings.

The rising and falling tide

The question of tidal rise and fall causes a fair amount of soul searching with some students, so I've decided to approach it as I did in my own learning – bit by bit. This should give your mind the chance to become accustomed to one level of knowledge before climbing up to the next. It helped me. I hope it will make it easier for you too. We'll look at the absolute basics here and now. In Chapter 6 we'll move further ahead, and by the time you've read Chapter 12, you'll know all you need to be fully on the pace.

Tide tables

There are so many harbours in the world, each with its own tidal characteristics, that to give every one its own tide tables would produce enough books to fill the average yacht saloon. This situation is handled by a system of 'standard' and 'secondary' ports. Tidal data are published annually for all standard ports. Each of these supports a catalogue of secondaries whose data vary predictably and regularly from their standard port. The necessary information appears in the nautical almanacs published annually and will be dealt with in detail later on. We'll make a start now by sorting out the matter of High and Low Water.

TIME ZONE (UT)
For Summer Time add ONE hour in **non-shaded areas**

ENGLAND – DARTMOUTH

LAT 50°21'N   LONG 3°34'W

TIMES AND HEIGHTS OF HIGH AND LOW WATERS

SEPTEMBER				OCTOBER				NOVEMBER			
Time	m	Time	m	Time	m	Time	m	Time	m	Time	m
1 0110	0.2	**16** 0041	0.6	**1** 0117	0.4	**16** 0048	0.5	**1** 0138	1.1	**16** 0148	0.9
0739	4.8	0713	4.7	0738	4.8	0720	4.9	0755	4.6	0822	4.9
W 1327	0.3	TH 1255	0.6	F 1331	0.6	SA 1306	0.6	M 1353	1.3	TU 1413	0.9
1950	5.0	1924	4.9	1948	4.8	1936	4.9	2008	4.4	2049	4.5
2 0148	0.3	**17** 0114	0.5	**2** 0147	0.7	**17** 0124	0.6	**2** 0200	1.4	**17** 0230	1.2
0815	4.7	0746	4.7	0805	4.7	0755	4.9	0823	4.5	0906	4.7
TH 1402	0.4	F 1328	0.6	SA 1400	0.8	SU 1340	0.7	TU 1416	1.5	W 1459	1.2
2024	4.9	1957	4.8	2013	4.6	2012	4.8	2039	4.1	2137	4.3

▶ Fig 3.2 Tide Table extract reproduced from the **Reeds Nautical Almanac**.

If you're lucky, your local harbour will be a standard port with the information immediately available in the almanac. If not, ask the harbourmaster or the chandler for a set of local tide tables. These cost only pennies and are quick and easy to use. The times of High and Low Water on a particular date are obvious. There are only two things to remember:

- Make sure you are reading the time correctly. Don't forget that in Britain we have BST and GMT or UT (Universal Time) to be politically correct. Some tide tables are corrected for the change. Others are not. There will be a note somewhere to this effect.

- You'll notice that High and Low Water are given in metres. These are the 'tidal heights' at which the water will stand at these times above chart datum. Low Water is generally a positive figure which means that, even at the bottom of the tide, there is almost always a greater depth than that given on the chart – a further safety factor if you are opting to work initially from the charted depth only. If you want a better idea of the real depth, you'll at least know what it is at High and Low Water times. If you're halfway between the two, it'll be very approximately midway between the two figures. If you're playing it safe with depth, leaving wide margins for error, this is enough information to take a cautious look outside.

AIDS TO NAVIGATION

Most charts show a number of permanently established aids to navigation. Many of these will have a lozenge-shaped magenta 'flash' attached to them, indicating that they are lit after dark with some unambiguous signal. Light characteristics are of no concern to you yet, but lit marks can often be seen blinking even in daylight from close range, so noting their characteristic and comparing this with the chart is a painless way to learn before you need to. Any sound signals such as bells or whistles on buoys and foghorns on lighthouses or pier heads are also spelled out in shorthand form. Refer to Chart 5011 (page 32, 'chart symbols') to check the details.

There may be a lighthouse or two, denoted by a small star with a code of letters and numbers giving details of its height, its light characteristics and whether it has a fog signal. More important for short-range pilotage are beacons and buoys.

Buoys will be one of a number of shapes as they float to the moorings that secure them to the bottom. They can be of lattice or solid in construction. They

▶ A full-size main channel marker – leave to port when inbound.

might look enormous close up – they can even be buoy-shaped structures placed in flat, open boats up to 25ft long – or they could be as small as a 10-gallon oil can painted up by a local harbour authority as a privately run mark. Beacons are generally posts set in the sea bed, but in some areas they might be substantial cairns built up like small towers. Sometimes a beacon takes the form of three or four posts joined together near the top, known as dolphins, and given the symbol 'Dn' with a tiny square.

Buoys appear on charts as mini-versions of their reality. Their colour is noted alongside them, either 'R' (red), 'G' (green), 'RGR'/'GRG' (red, green, red green, red, green etc.), 'Y' (yellow), 'RW' (red and white), 'BRB' (black, red, black) or 'BY' (black over yellow). Where one colour is above the other on a two-coloured buoy, the upper one is mentioned first.

Lateral marks

These are either red or green. They denote the presence of a deepwater channel and might be either beacons or buoys. Depending on how deep this actually is, they may or may not be of interest to you, but your chart will make the answer clear. Some channels are for big ships, with plenty of water for small craft on either side; in which case yachts are well advised to keep clear if shipping is using them.

▶ A small, unlit channel marker – starboard hand.

Although there are times when you will ignore them as irrelevant, red marks, whether buoys or beacons, are generally kept on your port side ('left to port') when moving up towards a harbour. Greens are left to starboard. A red mark generally carries a cylindrical topmark the same sort of shape as a baked bean tin, although it may taper towards its upper end. For this reason, red buoys are known as 'cans'. Green lateral marks have pointed topmarks and are more often than not conical in shape, hence 'cones'.

Later in your career, you will occasionally come across lateral buoys out at sea where no harbour is in the vicinity to indicate which side to pass. The answer to this conundrum is to read

▶ A beacon marking the port-hand side of the channel inbound.

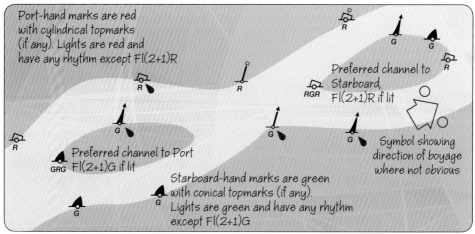

Port-hand marks are red
with cylindrical topmarks
(if any). Lights are red and
have any rhythm except Fl(2+1)R

Preferred channel to
Starboard,
Fl(2+1)R if lit

Symbol showing
direction of boyage
where not obvious

Preferred channel to Port
Fl(2+1)G if lit

Starboard-hand marks are green
with conical topmarks (if any).
Lights are green and have any rhythm
except Fl(2+1)G

▶ Fig 3.3 Lateral marks

the chart, be grateful that they exist as a means of establishing your position and don't worry yourself about why they are coloured as they are.

The favoured channel mark

These are rare, but they do form part of the lateral system. Where a channel divides, one of the two is often preferred for deeper-draught vessels. The distinction may only be relevant to a supertanker, but in some circumstances it could matter to you. Common sense and a reading of the chart will tell you. Whether buoy or beacon, a favoured channel mark is striped horizontally green and red. If the top section is red with a red topmark, leave it to port if it matters. If green with a green conical topmark, those requiring the deeper channel will treat it as a starboard-hand marker.

Cardinal marks

A cardinal mark represents a different approach to marking dangers, but one which is in common use throughout northern Europe. It may occasionally be found on the side of a channel, but more often it is sited to one side or another of an obstruction. There are four types of cardinal mark, each named for a cardinal point of the compass, north, south, east or west. A north cardinal mark stands to the north of the danger, and so on. Thus, if you see a north cardinal and cannot find it on the chart to check whether it concerns you directly or not, you should pass north of it, safe in the knowledge that it is between you and whatever it is marking.

Cardinal marks are black and yellow. The disposition of their colours and the shape of their topmarks is easy to remember. The topmarks consist of various types of double arrowhead pointer which mnemonics make unmistakable:

North: Both topmark arrows point upwards – main body of the beacon or buoy has its black at the top. The yellow, by default, is at the bottom. Symbol, BY. Mnemonic: 'North points north'

South: Topmarks both point downwards – black at the bottom, yellow at the top (YB).
Mnemonic: 'South points south'

East: Topmarks point outwards (two triangles with their bases together disposed 'up-and-down') – black at top and bottom, yellow in the middle (BYB).
Mnemonic: 'Looks like a classical letter "e" with a mirror image' or an egg

West: Topmarks point inwards ('up-and-down') – black in the middle, yellow at top and bottom (YBY).
Mnemonic: 'West Winds Wool' (looks like an old-fashioned bobbin), or, if you prefer, 'Wasp-Waisted Woman' – all the 'W's for West (Fig 3.4).

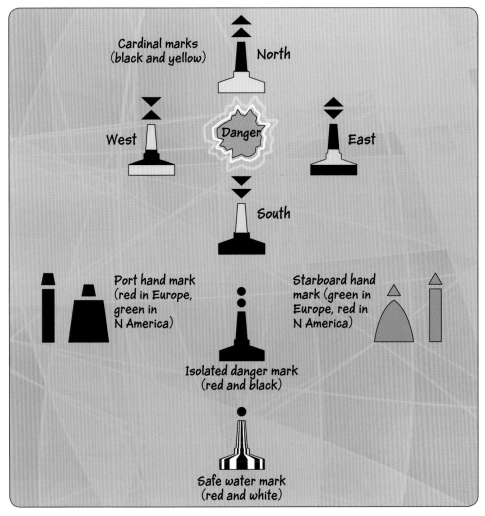

▶ Fig 3.4 Navigation marks.

Isolated dangers

These are marked by buoys or beacons horizontally striped red and black with two spherical topmarks one above the other. I have a private mnemonic for these two balls up in the air, but it is sadly unprintable. Use your imagination and you'll never forget . . .

Safe water marks

You'll often find one of these in the approaches to a harbour. It sits in deep water and can safely be passed either side. Look for vertical red and white stripes and a round, red topmark.

▶ A south cardinal buoy. It is yellow at the top and black below, as indicated by the topmarks – pass south of it and you will clear its danger.

▶ An east cardinal beacon with schematic black and yellow marking on its pile; topmarks 'pointing' to black at top and bottom.

Special marks

These yellow markers can be all manner of shapes. Unless for racing, they are rarely of direct navigational importance to yachts. Their topmarks are 'x' shapes. If you should see a buoy shaped like a port or starboard-hand marker and can't find it on the chart to make an informed decision, leave it to the appropriate side just to be sure.

Wreck markers

Wrecks are usually marked by cardinal buoys sited all round them. A new wreck that is not yet fully established is marked with blue-and-yellow buoys. They even flash alternate blue and yellow after dark.

▶ A blue and yellow buoy indicates a wreck that hasn't yet received its full complement of cardinal markers.

Chart symbols

All yachts using Admiralty charts should carry a copy of Admiralty Chart 5011. This is actually a booklet, and it is the bible for chart symbols, of which there are so many that few yachtmasters come close to knowing even half of them. If you don't have a copy, check through an Admiralty Small Craft Folio. One of the charts will often have some basic chart symbols shown on the reverse side.

Many chart symbols are self-explanatory, such as those for buoys, radio masts, chimneys, churches, bridges and wrecks. Note that floating buoys are always shown at a jaunty angle, while beacons stand vertical.

Rocks

Probably the most common danger, rocks have a number of symbols to mark their position. Running aground on sand is unpleasant and on mud it's a nuisance, but even in sheltered waters, on rocks it might be terminal, so give them a wide, wide berth (Fig 3.5).

Rocks

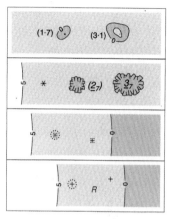

▶ Fig 3.5 Chart symbols.

VENTURING OUT OF HARBOUR

You now have enough essential pilotage and boat handling information to leave your berth, motor out of harbour and note how the chart shapes up to the three-dimensional reality out there. If you know how to sail, this is also a good time to pull up the canvas and see how the boat performs, but I'm holding that back for the next chapter because there are still one or two more skills for a beginner to master before taking up the challenge of the rig.

Take a close look at the chart to check which way you should be going, and what you're likely to encounter in the way of navigation aids. If possible beforehand, walk or drive over to a vantage point and familiarise yourself with the scene at the entrance. Perhaps make a few notes about what you expect to see and do, then it's back to Chapter 2, picking once again a good time for tidal movement past the berth. Hoist the ensign, take a look over the side to check the current, see how this relates to the tide tables to know what it's likely to be doing when you return, assess the breeze and get under way.

As soon as you encounter your first boat you'll realise that you must know how to react. Do you turn to port or starboard to avoid a head-on collision? What happens if someone is overtaking you? Must you really give way to boats under sail? In general, just who gives way to whom, and how? Not only is it potentially dangerous not to know the answers to these questions, it will also make you feel stupid. Fortunately, the Rule of the Road at sea is universally accepted, applied and, for a small yacht, blessedly simple.

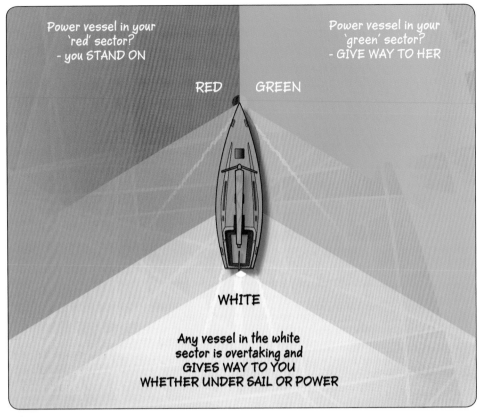

Power vessel in your
'red' sector?
- you STAND ON

Power vessel in your
'green' sector?
- GIVE WAY TO HER

RED   GREEN

WHITE

Any vessel in the white
sector is overtaking and
GIVES WAY TO YOU
WHETHER UNDER SAIL OR POWER

▶ Fig 3.6 Collision regulations for powered vessels.

The collision regulations (Colregs) break down into a few definable situations under power, plus one or two extra when you are sailing. We'll deal with the sailing tomorrow. Here's how it works under engine (Fig 3.6):

The International Regulations for Preventing Collision at Sea

Boats under power meeting head-on

This one's easy. Both vessels turn to starboard and pass 'port side to port side'. The rule for travelling along a channel is really only an extension of this. Within the bounds of common sense, all vessels should 'drive on the right' when others are in the vicinity, so that they pass 'port to port'.

One boat overtaking another

Here's another simple one. The overtaking vessel keeps clear, whether she is under sail, power or even oars.

Vessel approaching your starboard side

If it were dark, you would be showing a green light to starboard and a red to port ('port wine red'). Your boat will have navigation lights even if you're not ready to use them, so if you forget this aide-mémoire, go forward and check. Remember this and crossing vessels cease to be a problem. Anyone seeing your green light – ie coming in on your starboard side – has right of way. 'See green and go.' As likely as not, you'd also be seeing his red light, which speaks for itself.

Vessel approaching your port side

This chap is seeing your red side so, just as if it were a traffic light, he must give way and you are the 'stand-on' vessel.

Just for the record, the red and green lights shine from dead ahead to a point 22½° abaft the relevant beam. If a vessel is in either of these sectors, it is crossing. If it's further aft than that, it's overtaking. In practice, ambiguity about whether a boat is 20° or 23° abaft your beam rarely arises, but if in doubt, give way in good time.

And that's it, except for a vessel actually under sail alone (not motor-sailing). Unless she's overtaking you, you must keep clear of her.

When to apply the rules

It's important to assess whether another vessel coming your way is really a collision risk or not. If she isn't, don't go jinking all round the ocean trying to avoid her. If it's your right of way, you are in any case obliged to stand on firmly. The only exception to this is if the give-way vessel is clearly not taking her responsibilities seriously and is leaving things too late for your comfort. It then becomes everybody's duty to do what they can to avoid collision. At such a time, you should consider taking way off as an alternative to turning. Often this is a better means of defusing a collision situation than a last-minute swerve which can end with both parties locked in a deathly series of abortive, self-cancelling dodges.

The best answer to collision situations, and the one recommended in the rules, is to take action early and decisively. If you are in the slightest doubt about what might happen, deal positively with the matter long before it becomes an issue. If you should officially have been standing on, the other skipper might think you slightly odd, but better that than some misunderstanding that could lead to disaster.

SKIPPER'S TIP   'MIGHT IS RIGHT'

Except when a large commercial vessel is constrained in her ability to manoeuvre by, for example, a channel, all ships and boats are theoretically bound equally by these rules. In practice, it is often unreasonable for you to press your case against a larger ship. Especially in confined waters, therefore, always give way to anything that is substantially heftier than you. When a vessel's size is on the borderline (a large yacht, for example) and you decide to give way to her regardless of your theoretical rights, do it early and do it obviously, so that the other skipper is in no doubt as to your intentions.

Recognising a potential collision situation

It isn't always immediately obvious that a collision risk exists, but as soon as another vessel looks as though she might be a concern you must find out. The only sure-fire system is once again to use the transit. Line the other fellow up against some feature in the background; if he's coming closer while not moving relative to it, he is on what is known as 'a steady bearing' and bound in for a crunch. The technique is identical to the one you've been using to check drift as you approach your berth. It's the usual story. Boats are not always going where they are pointing.

Where there's no definable background, keep a steady course and site the opposition over a useful feature of your own boat. A stanchion is favourite. If she stays sitting on it as she approaches, it's time to apply the rules. Do you give way or stand on?

Out at sea, it's possible to note the compass bearing of a distant ship and, if it remains the same over a period of time, you're inbound for collision. On inshore passages it's rare to have to go to these lengths. Rules of thumb are more relevant.

▶ A big ship steaming your way can be an alarming sight, but so long as you steer to keep her bearing changing, there's nothing to worry about.

THE WIDE BLUE YONDER

Now that you're squared away about meeting other boats and yachts, it's safe to motor out of harbour. The purpose of this exercise is to break the bogey by not being too ambitious, to spend some time familiarising yourself with how the chart relates to reality and to get used to your immediate locality.

Pick a quiet day when the sea is not going to be rough and steer to a safe position well clear outside. Now stop, or motor slowly in one direction and bring the chart out on deck. So long as you make absolutely sure it can't blow away, there is no harm in this. I do it so often that I even have a dedicated clear plastic bag to keep it dry in bad weather. Look around, note navigational marks and shore features, then relate them to the chart. Now find some charted object that you haven't yet spotted and try to see it for real. Assess where you think you are, note the likely depth from the chart, make a 'ball-park' mental arithmetic adjustment for tide and look at your echo sounder. Does the depth reading add up? If so, you have one solid source of data that suggests you might be where you think you are. If not, take a closer look at the chart, decide whether the error could be down to the fact that you aren't too hot on tides yet, and think again. To double-check your tide height, toddle over to a known location, perhaps beside an unambiguous navigation buoy with a convenient sounding close by.

Compare the echo sounder with the chart. Any difference is the tide. Does it stack up now?

Don't get too bogged down over depth. It is only one item on your list. Remember that the main purpose of your outing is familiarisation with the chart. A good session like this on a clear day can be worth many hours in the classroom. When you're satisfied you've extracted all you can from the trip, motor back to your berth, run out lines and fenders, put the kettle on if it's not yet cocktail time and sit quietly in the cockpit to consider what you've learned.

Don't forget to lower the ensign at sunset once more. If you have small children, give them the job, and put them in charge of fenders too. There are always plenty of people who will come sailing with you on a sunny day, but a family that really works the ship as a team, sharing out the responsibilities, tends to go on sailing together for many happy years.

4

BEGINNING TO SAIL AS A SKIPPER

As with the section on power handling, if you can already sail well you might choose to skip this session, but I recommend that you read through it all the same, if only to reassure yourself that you are not developing any misconceptions. It is not unusual to do this, particularly among the self-taught. The chapter is structured so as to make sure you understand the mechanics of how it all works before moving on to the practice.

● THEORY OF SAIL

Aerodynamics

Most of the time, a sail doesn't actually push the boat along. It is not flat, but curved like the wing of an aeroplane and acts as an aerofoil just as a wing does. Aerofoils lift themselves more or less vertically to an airstream. As an aircraft moves down the runway, it creates an airflow across the wing which begins to lift upwards. The force increases with speed until it becomes greater than the weight of the aeroplane, which then takes off.

If you think of a sail as a wing made of cloth, set vertically instead of horizontally, you'll see that its power must be delivered sideways across the surface of the sea, rather than upwards. A sail's relationship to the fore-and-aft midline of the boat is controlled by ropes called sheets. Since, like a wing, its power is delivered more or less square across it, the further the sail can be allowed to swing out across the boat, the greater will be its forward drive.

When the sheet is eased too far, the sail will start to blow inside out at its leading edge. This condition is called 'lifting' – a potentially confusing term that has nothing whatever to do with the aerodynamic lift of the sail. If allowed to lift excessively, it will ultimately flap as air blows evenly down both sides and the sail cannot make up its mind which way to set. Pull the sheet in to sort it out. If, on the other hand, the sail is pulled in too close to the midline for the boat's angle to the wind, not only does it tend to force the boat sideways and make her heel* more than is necessary,

▶ A typical set of modern yacht jammers. These are sited aft near the cockpit so all the ropes can be worked, one at a time, from a single winch.

▶ A reefed in-mast mainsail won't pull as well as a slab-reefed equivalent, but so long as you keep the tensions right, it will deliver what you need.

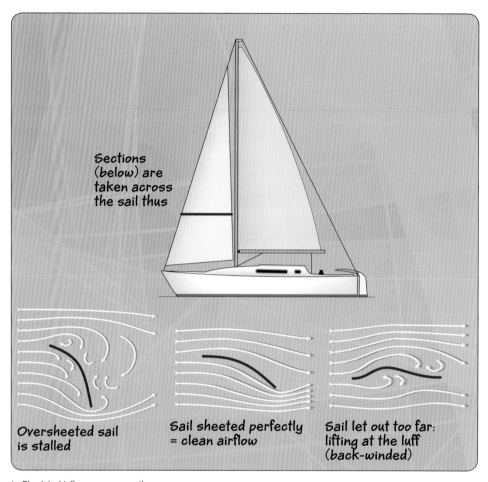

Sections
(below) are
taken across
the sail thus

Oversheeted sail
is stalled

Sail sheeted perfectly
= clean airflow

Sail let out too far:
lifting at the luff
(back-winded)

▶ Fig 4.1 Airflow across a sail.

it 'stalls' so that the airstream no longer flows sweetly across it. This condition is cured by easing out the sheet.

The upshot of all this is that whatever angle a boat is making to the wind, the sail should be 'sheeted' so as to set as far out as it can without lifting or flapping (Fig 4.1).

The points of sailing

There are two ways of defining the direction a boat is taking. One is in terms of the compass course she is steering. The other is an expression of the angle she is making with the wind.

Leaving the question of compass courses to one side for the moment, it's obvious even to a child that a sailing boat can blow downwind. Most people have no difficulty with the idea of her sailing across the wind, either, it's making progress directly against it that baffles the uninitiated. The diagram (Fig 4.2) analyses the various conditions or 'points of sailing' in which a yacht can find herself. The number she sets makes no difference to her point of sailing, however, so we'll work with a single sail to keep it simple, noting what is going on in theory and what the crew must do to make it all happen.

The beam reach

This is the easiest point of sailing. The wind is blowing square across the boat and her keel is stopping her from being pushed sideways. The sail can be sheeted well out to produce lots of forward drive.

Broad reach

The most comfortable angle of all. With the wind coming from abaft the beam, the sail is eased all the way out until it presses against the shrouds and can go no further. Drive is thus optimised, with heeling at a minimum.

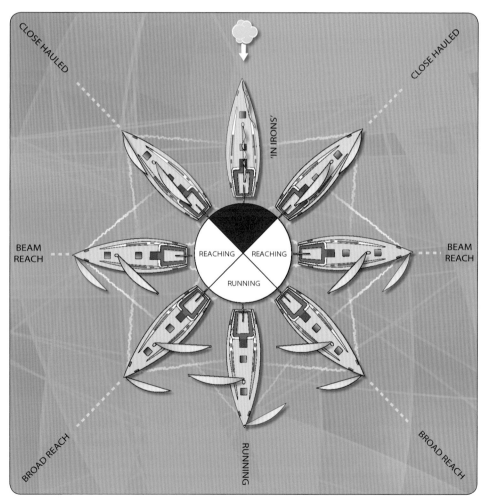

▶ Fig 4.2 The points of sailing.

Running

Running downwind, the sail is still all the way out, but because the wind is hitting it at right angles, it is well and truly stalled. In a cruising yacht, running is often slower than reaching because the sail generates less power for a given wind strength when pushing than it does when it is lifting.

Gybing

As the boat turns steadily away from the wind, there comes a point when her course alteration takes it across her stern. You'll have noticed that the sail always sets on the downwind, or leeward side of the boat. The process as it crosses to the new lee side is called 'gybing'. It can be dramatic if the sail is allowed to take charge on a windy day, or it may be docile in any weather if executed by a well-trained crew.

The 'no-go zone' and closehauled sailing

As you steer ever closer to the direction of the wind, you will pass the beam reach and the close reach, sheeting the sail in progressively until it arrives at a point where you can't haul it in any further. If you try to steer closer to the wind, the sail will start lifting. The only corrective action you can take is with the helm, by steering a few degrees away from the wind so that the airstream is once again presented to the sail effectively. Because you can do nothing more with the sheet, you are now effectively setting the sail with the helm. Steer 'too high' (too close to the breeze) and the sail lifts, the boat comes upright and loses way. Bear away* (steer further off the wind than the close-sheeted sail would like) and the sail stalls, the boat slows down once more, but this time she heels more than she should. When the helmsman is steering right 'in the groove', the boat is said to be 'sailing closehauled'. For most boats, the angle is somewhere around 45° from the true direction of the wind.

If you're closehauled, yet your destination still lies to windward of your course, you cannot get there by direct sailing. It's therefore in your 'no-go zone'. The only way into this area is by tacking (Fig 4.3).

Tacking to windward

To work up to a point inside the no-go zone you must 'beat to windward'. If sea-room were no problem and the wind absolutely steady, you'd sail closehauled up one edge of the no-go zone until the destination was exactly abeam (90°) across the wind. Then you'd turn your bow through the wind and keep turning until the close-sheeted sail filled on the other side. You'd now have turned through a right angle and your destination would lie ahead. This process of turning the yacht's head through the wind is called 'tacking', or 'going about'.

The business of working a boat to windward, tack by tack, because you cannot initially 'lay' your objective is known as 'beating'. Sometimes, land or other obstructions prevent you from sailing one tack until you can 'lay' the objective after going about. When this happens, as it often does in rivers or areas such as the Solent or the Sound of Mull, the yacht must make several tacks to move herself upwind.

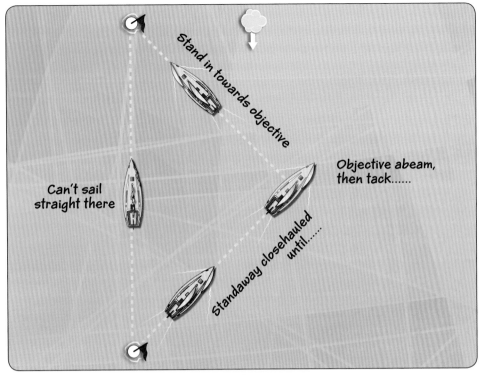

Stand in towards objective

Objective abeam, then tack......

Can't sail straight there

Standaway closehauled until......

▶ Fig 4.3 Beating to an objective dead to windward.

● FIRST STEPS UNDER SAIL

If you've already been crewing for someone else, you might be surprised at how many small decisions have thus far been made without your direct input. Now it's all down to you. A classic case is what instructors and examiners call 'wind awareness'.

Wind awareness

It should be axiomatic that a sailor knows where the wind is coming from, yet surprisingly large numbers do not. I know this from my work as an examiner, and I put it down to not mastering the subject from the outset.

When a boat travels through the water, she is also moving through the air, creating her own headwind. This exists regardless of conditions, whether sailing in a gale or motoring in flat calm. That's why it always seems windy on a ferry, even on a still day. This headwind affects the true wind that is blowing across the water, creating a composite airstream aboard the yacht called the 'apparent wind'. It is in this that the boat sails.

For example, when you have a beam wind, the residual air blowing from ahead will cause the breeze over your deck to move a few degrees forward of the true wind. It adds its own velocity to winds from forward of the beam, making them a little stronger than the true wind, and subtracts from following winds, creating a false aura of relative peace when running. The apparent wind is what you feel on your cheek, what an uncorrected instrument senses and reads out, what on-board flags fly to and what your sails use to drive the boat.

Most of the time, a sailor's interest centres on the apparent wind, but when you are making a tactical decision – when to go about for example – you must identify the true wind. Here's how to do both:

- **True wind** Check flags ashore, smoke rising from chimneys or anchored ships, or anything else static that is reacting to the flowing air. If nothing presents itself, take a long look at the water from your deck, noting the small wind ripples (not the bigger waves) which are created by the breeze just as you make them yourself when you breathe across a bowl of soup. The wind is blowing at right angles across them. They aren't easy to spot at first, but it's well worth training your eye, because under way offshore, or even up a creek with no other signs visible, they're all you've got.

- **Apparent wind** Everything on board while you are under way registers apparent wind. Closehauled, you'll see that the burgee*, windex* or instruments all suggest you're sailing 35° or so from the wind. So you are, but it's only the apparent wind which is shifted ahead by the boat's motion through the air. Unless you're in a hotshot racer, you're still sailing a few degrees more or less than 45° from the true wind, so don't expect to tack through 70°. It'll be the good old right-angle if you're lucky, the same as it is for the rest of us!

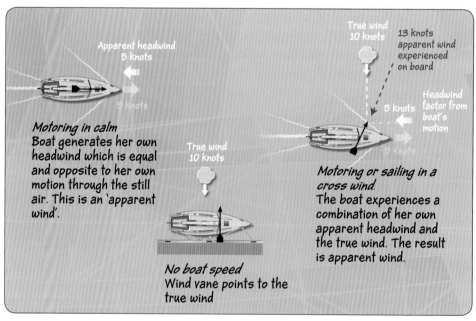

Apparent headwind
5 knots

Motoring in calm
Boat generates her own headwind which is equal and opposite to her own motion through the still air. This is an 'apparent wind'.

True wind
10 knots

No boat speed
Wind vane points to the true wind

True wind
10 knots

13 knots
apparent wind
experienced
on board

Headwind
factor from
boat's
motion

5 knots

Motoring or sailing in a cross wind.
The boat experiences a combination of her own apparent headwind and the true wind. The result is apparent wind.

▶ Fig 4.4 Apparent wind.

- **Feeling the wind** You'll hear people talking about feeling the wind 'on the back of their necks'. I've never managed to do this with any degree of accuracy other than to note that it's making me cold, but I can feel it on my face and assess its direction to better than 5°. Slip off your hood and turn down your collar to receive the full benefit. Now face the breeze, make sure nobody's looking and wag your head slowly from side to side. You'll feel the wind cross your nose quite sharply – I reckon it's my earlobes or my cheeks that are picking it up. Now turn your head less and less until both sides are delivering the same message. At this point you're exactly facing the wind. Try it. It's amazingly accurate. It reads true wind if you're not under way, apparent any other time.

Wind-spotting ability becomes more important as your boat handling gains in sophistication, so start now.

SAILS AND WINCHES

Before going out for a sail, your first job after making sure the weather is what you want, is to select and bend on your canvas. If this is already dealt with by self-furling systems, so much the easier.

The mainsail

Most modern yachts keep their mainsails permanently attached to the mast and boom or, as the proper terminology has it, 'bent on'. This can be done in a number of ways, so take a constructive look at yours in case anything should ever go wrong. You'll find it's largely a matter of common sense.

Battens

The leech* of nearly every mainsail, except the in-mast self-stowing variety, is stiffened by battens of wood or a composite material. These run forward from the leech and are held in place by 'pockets'. Inspect them for wear and check how they work.

Outhaul

The tension of the foot of a mainsail is important to its set. Methods of achieving this vary. Some sails are just lashed out to an eye on the aft end of the boom. With others, the clew* runs on a car* in a slot and is controlled by an 'outhaul' line. This leads aft from the clew to a sheave* in the boom end then forward, generally inside the boom, to a jammer*. Whatever system you find, the tension is best set at a solid medium to start with. Pull the clew out until any suggestion of 'up-and-down' wrinkles disappears from the foot of the sail when hoisted. If the foot starts developing a deep 'fore-and-aft' wrinkle, you have pulled it harder than you need at this stage.

Sheet

Mainsheets almost invariably develop their extra power by means of a tackle*. In theory, if four parts of the rope are running out of the moving block* (the one on

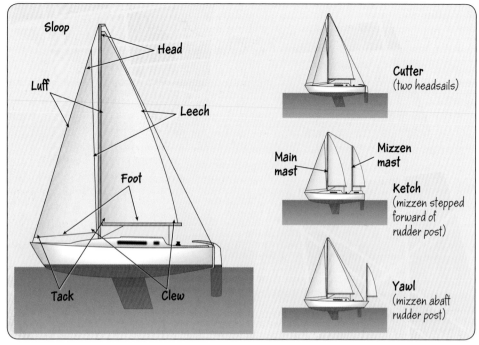

▶ Fig 4.5 Parts of a sail.

the boom), you have a 4:1 advantage. Some of this is lost in friction, particularly if the rope is too big for the sheaves or stiff with age, as is often the case, but the tackle certainly helps. Occasionally, the sheet runs from the middle of the boom rather than the end. This is a less efficient arrangement which often results in a winch being provided to heave in the sheet. Always tie a figure-eight knot at the extreme end of any sheet, so that you cannot lose it.

Halyard

A halyard* is a rope dedicated to hoisting a particular sail. The main halyard is generally stowed away from the sail, or at least taken under a mast winch or cleat to stop it slatting noisily against the mast at rest and prevent the luff* riding up the forestay before you are ready to hoist. Once it has been disconnected or led 'foul' in this way, the slack is taken up so that the halyard is neatly stowed. To make it ready, either shackle it to the head of the sail or clear it from its impediments. In either case, always look aloft to make sure everything is untangled. The hauling end will either come down outside the mast (rarely nowadays) or, more likely, appear through a port either near the deck or above the mast winches.

Kicking strap, or Vang

This is the name given to the tackle running between the mast at deck level and the forward part of the boom. Its job is to help keep the boom at the correct angle

▶ A powerful spring-loaded kicker, but note what a bad lead the rigger has given the purchase. The blocks should be the other way around. Always check leads to make sure there is no friction.

for good sail shape by holding the spar down against its natural tendency to kick up skywards. Some larger yachts have a hydraulically augmented vang instead of the simple tackle. This may well be adjusted with a block system, like its humbler counterpart. However it is controlled, it will serve the additional purpose of preventing the boom from falling too low under its own weight, thus rendering the topping lift (see below) at least partially redundant.

Topping lift

On a boat with no hydraulic boom vang, there would be nothing to stop the outboard end of the boom falling into the cockpit when the sail is lowered, were it not for the topping lift. The topping lift is a simple line running from the boom end to the masthead, round a turning block and back to a cleat on the mast or to a jammer in some more convenient spot. Before dropping the main, the topping lift is 'made up' to prevent the boom braining the crew. After the sail is hoisted, it is eased away to allow the boom to take up its natural attitude.

Stowing a mainsail

The quickest way to stow the main is by having all the sail fall on one side, hauling the leech aft and, starting at the foot, throwing the sail into the natural bag formed between the foot and the boom. Keep hauling aft as you stow. Finish off by rolling the whole lot tightly on top of the boom and tying it securely.

▶ Two modern mainsail systems – a stack-pack (foreground) with an in-mast main behind it.

An alternative method, said to be kinder to a stiff sail, is to 'flake' it. Once again, all the sail starts on one side and the leech is hauled aft. Take a couple of feet of the leech and heave it over to the other side of the boom. Hold the flake thus formed in place and repeat the process until the sail has been folded like a concertina. Tie it down and, if you have a sail cover, put it on once you're back in your berth. A flaked sail rarely looks as tasty as a well rolled one, but if the sail is still new you may have little choice.

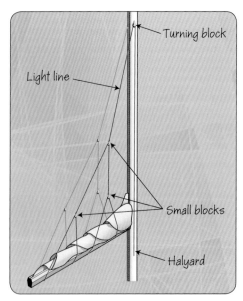

▶ Fig 4.6 Lazy jacks are a great way to control a mainsail when lowering it. This type can be eased and taken forward out of the way on a longer passage by letting off the halyard.

▶ This stack-pack mainsail does not have the benefit of full-length battens, so the skipper is heaving the leech aft as the sail comes down to keep things tidy.

Stack-packs and lazy jacks

A stack-pack is a permanently rigged sail cover on the main boom, into which the sail falls naturally when dropped. It has the huge advantage of doing away with people having to totter around on the coach roof when stowing the sail at sea in rough weather. It also makes covering it as easy as pie. The cover is held 'up' by a system of light lines from the spreaders called 'lazy jacks'. The name means what it says. Jolly Jack the sailorman, or Jackie his sister, can sit back lazily and watch as the sail falls between these cunningly contrived arrangements into the stack pack. All that remains is for them to zip up the bag and pour the drinks.

Such systems often make use of fully-battened mainsails, which carry giant battens running all the way from luff to leech. They help the sail self-stow. They also shape it positively, but nothing at sea comes for free and they can create problems when the sail is dropped or hoisted if the boat is not head to wind. Such systems don't always work quite as they do in the advertisements, but with practice and care they are remarkable labour-savers.

In-mast furling mainsails

These allow the sail to be set or winched away into the mast via a slot in the spar. Neat, effective and, on the whole, reliable. Just make sure you know how the gear works in case there's ever a problem.

Headsails

'Headsail' is the name given to any sail set forward of the mast. A small one is known as a 'jib', while bigger ones that overlap the mast when sheeted home are called 'genoas'. There are three basic systems of dealing with headsails:

- **Foils** Race boats set their headsails from grooves running up an aerodynamic aluminium extrusion built into the forestay. If you come across one of these 'foils', you have only to hook on the tack, guide the head of the luff into the 'feeder' (a device attached on deck near the bow that floats free on a short lanyard) then into the groove, bend on the halyard and hoist away. Keep such a sail bagged until you need it however, because they are the devil to control on deck if a breeze gets up.

- **Hanked-on headsails** Until the early 1980s, most cruiser headsails were attached to the forestay with piston hanks. Sails like this are stowed below in bags and you must select the one you want, often out of a choice of three or four. Unless it is very light air, choose a working jib for your first outing (No 2 or 3). Attach the tack first, usually with a snap shackle. Next, work your way up the luff towards the head, snapping on one hank after the next and making sure they are all the same way round. The halyard will be stowed somewhere nearby, often on the pulpit*, ready to be attached when the time comes to hoist the sail. Don't clip it on before you are ready, because it will tend to drag the sail up the stay by the halyard's weight. If you do attach it, you will have to tie the head down some- how, which is another job. It's a lot easier just to make shackling on the halyard the last item before hoisting, and detaching it first when you drop the sail.

- **Roller furlers** By far the most common arrangement for a cruising yacht is some sort of roller-furling device for a permanently bent-on genoa. The sail is set from a groove rather like a race foil, but the whole device is rotated to furl the sail away. It can also be partly rolled to shorten its area in stronger winds. To deploy the sail, you'll find a 'furling line' which is progressively released as the sheet is hauled out. The line may be on a winch but is more usually led straight to a jamming cleat in the cockpit. Don't just let this run to open the sail. If you do, it won't reel away neatly and may even foul. Ease it out as you haul in the sheet.

  A roller-furling headsail can be hoisted or lowered like a foil sail but is generally left up on its stay all season.

Headsail sheets

Unless you have a roller-furling headsail, one job when bending on a headsail is attaching the sheets. These are generally two individual braidlines of between 10mm and 14mm diameter, one each side. Bend them onto the sail with bowline knots, then lead them through their fairleads*. These are generally found mounted on adjustable 'cars' running on aluminium tracks on the side deck abaft the shrouds. The natural sheeting route on most boats passes outboard of the rigging, thence to the biggest winches at the cockpit (known as the primaries), often by way of a turning block close to the winch. After the sheet has passed through all its blocks, tie a figure-eight knot in the extreme aft end so that it cannot unreeve* itself.

▶ The figure-eight stopper knot is used to prevent headsail sheets from unreeving.

To leave the sheets ready for use after bending them on, pass a couple of turns round the winches, pull through all the slack, make them fast with a half turn and a single figure of eight on the cleat by the winch, coil up the tails and hang them neatly over the winch barrels.

Winches

Today's mainstream yachts invariably have at least two sheet winches and often a number of others for cranking up halyards, reefing* and other functions. All these operate clockwise and rely on the friction of a number of 'turns' around the barrel to provide grip.

Winching in

Here's how to use a sheet winch, starting with the sheet off the barrel altogether.

- Take the sheet firmly but carefully in your hand, always bearing in mind that loads can suddenly increase and trap the fingers of the unvigilant.

- Pass it twice around the barrel, clockwise.

- Heave in the slack around the winch and watch the sail. If it needs to come in more, lean back on the sheet until you are not strong enough to pull it unaided then pass two more turns around the barrel.

- Holding the sheet as it comes off the winch with one hand, engage the handle in the top of the barrel with the other.

■ Maintain some pull on the sheet coming off the barrel to keep the friction on (this process is called 'tailing'), then wind the winch handle. If the winch is two-speed, try winding either way to find which is most appropriate. If the designer has specified the correct winches, you'll get most of the sheet in at low power (high speed) and then turn to high power for the final grunt. If you have a full crew and the winching is hard work, have someone tail for you and give the handle all you've got with both hands. Position your body over the barrel so you're looking straight down onto the winch. You'll never see a sailor operating a loaded winch at arm's length.

▶ Winching in – note how the sheet is loaded onto the self-tailing winch and that the crew has his body weight well over the winch barrel.

■ When you're satisfied with sail trim, cleat off with a round turn, a figure of eight and an extra half turn to hold the sheet in place.

Easing and releasing sheets from winches

Even a moderate breeze can generate a surprising load on the headsail sheets. To ease one out, first remove it from the self-tailer or cleat, making sure you keep some pressure on the tail to maintain the friction of the turns. Now place one hand on the turns and carefully but positively work them round the barrel, easing off the tension as you do so. You'll feel when the pressure is sufficiently reduced to be able to take off a turn or two. While still keeping control with the residual turns, it is now safe to ease more rapidly by letting the sail pull the sheet around the winch. See photo on page 61.

SKIPPER'S TIP	SELF-TAILING WINCHES

You'll recognise these by a sort of flat crown on the top of the barrel just the right size to take the bight of the sheet. Sheeting in, nothing changes in technique until you reach the winding stage. Then, instead of tailing, take the sheet once round the top of the barrel, sliding it into the grip of the self-tailing device. This will now hold it while you address all your energies to winding the handle. It can even be used to secure the sheet, but a line made fast by no more than the grip of the winch is subject to accidental release, so take another loose turn round the barrel just to make sure this doesn't happen.

To release a sheet suddenly, when you are tacking for example, ease off the worst of the pressure as described above, then rip the turns off the winch by pulling the sheet positively upwards. Watch it until it has run through to make sure it doesn't whip into a muddle. Remember, a rope that is given half a chance will always find a way to foul itself.

BASIC SAILING

Rule of the Road under sail

Now that you're sailing, a different set of rules applies in collision situations. These are straightforward and easy to memorise. The only new concept to come to terms with is that of which tack you are on. A yacht with the wind coming over her starboard side is on the starboard tack. Vice versa for port tack. Don't fall into the trap of imagining that when your boom is on the port side, you're 'on port'. You aren't. It's the windward side that makes the play.

The regulations themselves are simple:

- A yacht on *starboard tack* has right of way over a yacht on *port tack*.

- If both yachts are on the same tack, the windward boat must keep clear.

- A vessel under sail has *prima facie* right of way over one under power. However, this rule must be applied with humility and good sense. Don't expect a tanker to give way to you at all, don't push your luck with a fishing vessel hurrying home to tea, and never do anything to compromise a deep-draught vessel working in a narrow channel.

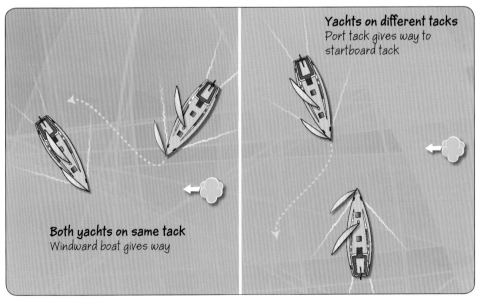

▶ Fig 4.7 Collision avoidance under sail.

■ If you are overtaking a powered vessel, you must keep clear, regardless of your sailing status.

Discovering the mainsail

If you are moored and lying head-to-wind, or your alongside berth happens to place you in this privileged position on the day, try hoisting and dropping the main before you leave. If you can't manage this, it's not the end of the world, because the next stage is to pull up the mainsail for real. Choose a day that is not too breezy, find yourself a stretch of quiet, deep water with room to manoeuvre, motor slowly head-to-wind, throw off the mainsail ties and hoist away. You don't have to be literally steering straight into the wind to hoist or drop the mainsail. Any wind direction will do, so long as it is far enough forward of the beam to allow the canvas to flap as it goes up or down with the sheet well eased. In the early stages, head-to-wind is a guaranteed safe option.

Before heaving on the halyard, check to see if anything might stop the sail going up freely. Two things almost certainly will do this if left untended: the mainsheet and the kicking strap, or 'kicker'. Ease both well off, 'overhauling'* a few feet of slack into the mainsheet just to make sure. The sail should now run sweetly. When it is nearly up, put two or three turns onto the halyard winch, if there is one, and wind up the last foot or two. Resist any temptation to pull the whole sail up with the halyard on the winch. It's noisy, annoying to others and wears out the winch pawls.

The question of how much tension to put onto the luff with the winch is best answered at this stage by heaving until a crease appears running up the luff. Now ease carefully until this just disappears, then let off the topping lift until just slack.

At this point, the sail will be banging around if there is more than the lightest of breezes. Still with the engine in gear, steer 90° to port or starboard so as to put the wind square across the boat. This is called wind 'abeam' and the boat is on a 'beam reach'. Ease the mainsheet until the sail starts to lift at the luff. Let it go even further so it flaps. Now pull it steadily in, keeping the boat straight, until it has just stopped lifting. Throw the engine into neutral and sail slowly along. The helm will then be unbalanced and you won't be going fast, but those first magic moments when the noise stops and the boat keeps right on going have been the defining ones of many lives.

▶ A tidily coiled and stowed halyard is secure and looks good too.

Now that things have quietened down, coil the halyard clockwise into your left hand, starting from where you have made fast so that any unwanted turns and kinks are thrown off the bitter end. When the coil is finished, hang it up as follows: holding the coil close to the cleat in your left hand, reach through it with your right and take hold of the halyard immediately it comes off the cleat. Pull a bight through the coil, twist it once and pass it over the top of the coil so that it just reaches the cleat. Now use this as a loop to hang the halyard onto the cleat. The weight of the coil will hold it there.

As soon as the halyard is tidy, bear away (turn more downwind) and ease the sheet, setting the sail properly. Next, luff up (come towards the wind) bit by bit, hauling in the sheet to keep the sail setting sweetly.

The business of attending to the sheets with every change of course is critical to good sailing, so it's as well to start as you mean to go on. Keep practising this, then note the point at which, when you have pulled the sail well in, it is still lifting. Glance at your masthead indicator and you'll see you are on the edge of the 'no-go zone'. If the boat hasn't stopped, demanding engine power to keep her moving again with the main pinned in and no headsail set as yet, bear away just enough to fill the sail and you're closehauled.

When you're ready, take a good look round to make sure you aren't about to alter course into someone else's path, engage the gears and run the engine slow ahead, then steer the bows firmly across the wind until the main fills on the other side. You have now tacked. Do this a few times to get the feel of things. If you find going about disorientating, choose a distant object 90° over your weather shoulder before you turn. Swing through the wind towards that, then fine-tune your heading after making the tack.

Main halyard tension

While you've been doing these exercises, you've had plenty of opportunity to study the sail. Any time it's full of wind, you can reassess the issue of halyard tension. Take a look at it now. Halyard tension should be set up so that any lateral creases disappear. If the halyard is not tight enough these will be notably prevalent in way of the luff sliders. The

▶ This mainsail needs a bit more kicker on in order to take some of the twist out of the leech. Note how the top batten is falling away. A bit more tension will pull it up so it's parallel with the boom.

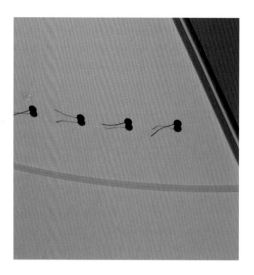

▶ A good set of tell-tales showing that this boat is bang in the groove sailing to windward. If a weather one starts to flick up, bear away a bit. If the shadow of the ones to leeward stops streaming cleanly, luff up to get back on track.

sail may even appear 'crinkle-cut' like a supermarket oven-ready potato chip. As before, heave away until that long vertical crease appears, then ease to get rid of it. You'll see people twanging the lower luff of their mainsails to assess tension and nodding sagely, as if to say, 'That's bang on.'

It might be, but you could only judge in this way after years of experience with a specific sail – and even then it is an arbitrary way of doing things. It could just as easily be too tight or too slack. The best way to decide is by observation.

Kicker tension and the mainsheet traveller

The same need to decide settings by observation is true for kicking strap ('kicker') tension. Once the sail is hoisted you must pull down on this. The simple way of judging the matter of how hard is to sight up the leech of the sail when the boat is on a close reach with the sheet eased. If the kicker is working properly, the top batten will more or less line up with the boom.

On most yachts, the lower mainsheet block runs on a traveller which can be adjusted athwartships by a tackle running across the boat. Misconceptions abound as to how this should be set. There's no rush, but when you're ready, read Chapter 5 to discover the details. In the meantime, or when in doubt, cleat it off in the centre.

Setting the headsail

The joy of all headsails is that they can be hoisted or lowered on any point of sailing. They don't have to flap and you certainly do not need to be head-to-wind.

Steer the boat onto a beam reach, trim the mainsheet, knock off the engine and hoist your headsail. If it's a roller, let out about two thirds. Sheet it in until it stops flapping. You'll be surprised at the difference it makes. Enjoy the feeling of sailing and don't be alarmed by the heeling. A boat always feels further over than she is. Re-assess the trim of the main. This may well need sheeting in a little as it is now being affected by the headsail.

▶ If you're using a self-tailing winch to secure a sheet and not a cleat, try to throw an extra turn around the top once you're finished winding to make sure nobody can accidentally knock the rope out of the jammer.

Slide the headsail sheet fairlead forward or aft (you may have to slacken the sheet right off to do this) so that if you sight up the sheet from the lead, it would cut the luff around one third of the way up. If you have woolly tell-tales stitched through your luff they should be streaming sweetly aft on both sides of the sail when it is correctly sheeted and the lead is in the right place. Adjust the car so that they all lift on the windward side together when the boat is steered too close to the wind from closehauled. If the top ones flip up first, move the lead forward, if the lower ones go, slide it aft but, whatever you do, remember that this is really a sophistication. The rule of thumb of 'one-third/two-thirds' will see you right for the time being.

● EXERCISES

When you're satisfied the boat is sailing nicely, have the crew ease the sheets, then bear away for a while. Now haul them hard in and come up closehauled. To decide how close in to heave a headsail, look aloft and winch in until the leech is a few inches off the spreader or the shrouds. Next, see if you can find the magic groove on the edge of the wind that will take you closest to an objective you cannot lay. Steer up too 'high' (windward tell-tales fly up) and you'll feel the boat lose power and come upright as the sails begin to lift. Bear away too far (lee side tell-tales go walkabout) and if you're concentrating you'll realise that you could be making a good deal more ground if you were closer to the wind.

Tack a few times, practising the techniques for letting go and sheeting in the jib, making sure the person on the helm doesn't come through the wind too fast. Ease her through and don't fall too far off on the new tack. So long as you can hold her at no more than 45° until the troops have winched in the genoa, they'll have an easy ride of it. Allow the boat to sag off onto a beam reach and you'll find them groping for the heart pills.

If you're feeling adventurous, bear right away onto a run. Don't worry when the headsail collapses. It's only because it is in the wind shadow of the main. Now turn dead downwind to set up for a gybe. Heave the mainsheet hard in to control the sail, and make it fast. Once it's secure, steer the stern through the wind. As soon as the boom has flipped across let the sheet away smartly, particularly if it's windy, because it will interfere drastically with your steering if you don't. Forget the jib while you gybe. When you have settled the main on the new side and all the action is over, pass the headsail across from one sheet to the other, keeping tension on both sheets as you do so. Letting the old one fly as you would when tacking can induce the sail to take a half-turn round the forestay – a pain you don't need. If you turn the stern across the wind without sheeting in, you are sailing 'by the lee' and may gybe involuntarily. This can be nasty on a windy day, so avoid it at all costs.

All through this session, keep relating what is happening to the theoretical 'points of sailing' diagram. If you can explain to yourself where you are on that circle at all times, you've cracked it. There may still be a lifetime of learning ahead, but the rest could be described as detail. Roll away the jib or drop and stow it, make sure no ropes are over the side lying in wait for the propeller, then start the engine and bring the boat head-to-wind. Motor slow ahead, lower the main, bundle it up, go home to your berth and celebrate.

5

SEAMANSHIP

Seamanship covers all manner of themes. In this book, I'm taking it to mean further depth on sail handling, rigging the boat to deal with stronger winds, certain important safety considerations and essential troubleshooting. All are subjects that must at least be understood before the boat puts to sea on passage.

● PREPARATION FOR SEA

I was once advised that before setting out on an ocean passage I should prepare my boat on the supposition that at some stage she would be turned upside down by a giant wave. For coastal passages this may be over the top, but the principle is a sound one. When stowing for any trip, it's sensible to assume that a sailing boat will be heeling to 30° and that just as a gust of wind hits her, so will the wash from the biggest high-speed motor yacht ever seen. A common coincidence like this will search out any laziness or muddled thinking.

Below, make sure all locker doors are properly closed, that nothing is left where it can slide onto the cabin sole, and that any heavy objects such as batteries are firmly secured. Go round and see that all opening lights, portholes and hatches are firmly dogged down. Check that seacocks to appliances that you know can siphon back are closed, pans are secure on the stove, books firmly wedged and that the First Aid kit is conveniently stowed and up-to-date.

On deck, see that any loose gear such as booming-out poles and boat hooks are safe. Warps* and fenders are to be stowed in their locker every time. If you're going to need foul weather gear or warm clothing, make sure it is handy so as to avoid a scrabble through bags or lockers when the boat is bouncing around.

In short, do all you can to prepare for the expected, the unexpected and the inevitable.

● DECK SAFETY

Moving around

It's a fine thing to be able to walk round a yacht as though you were in the back garden at home, but as soon as the sea chops up, you'll have to hang on. One of the oldest rules of the sea is, 'when working on deck or aloft, it's one hand for the ship and one for yourself.' Keep this always in the forefront of your mind, move forward on the weather, or 'high' side where there is any choice, and never hesitate to wear your safety harness. Unless you are a non-swimmer, in which case a lifejacket is essential on deck, you may feel it is more important to stay attached to the boat

▶ When working forward to the cockpit, a safety harness is best clipped to a jackstay running the length of the boat.

than to float if you fall off. After all, unless you're unconscious you can always swim. The ideal answer is for the harness to be integral with the lifejacket.

Safety harnesses

In the UK at least, no hard and fast rules exist about when these should be worn during a day sail. Night passages are not your problem at the moment, but once you start them you'll probably agree that nobody should leave the cockpit after dark without being clipped on. In daylight a better guide-line is quite simply, 'put it on when you feel you want it'.

If this is not precise enough, a useful pointer for crew on deck is to clip on in conditions where the boat would be carrying a reef if sailing closehauled.

Like modern lifejackets, today's safety harnesses are easy to wear so nobody need hesitate on grounds of inconvenience. Most yachts are fitted with webbing or coated wire 'jackstays' running fore-and-aft along the deck. Clip onto this before you leave the cockpit, then use your common sense. It's often possible to complete a task such as reefing without unclipping at all, but if needs must, wait for a calm patch, unhook the harness and remember, 'one hand for yourself and one for the ship'.

● MECHANICS OF STOWING HEADSAILS

Roller genoas

On the face of things, stowing or reefing a roller genoa is as simple as easing the sheet and heaving in on the furling line. And in very light weather, that's all there is to it. On a breezy day, however, especially with a bigger boat, hauling in the furling line can be a challenge. Except on the largest yachts, using a winch must be the final resort, and the last thing you want is to come head-to-wind.

The trick is to make sure you have plenty of sea room so that you can run away from the wind for a short while. At some stage well before the boat is on a dead run, the genoa will fall into the wind shadow of the mainsail. This completely defuses its efforts to make your life a misery. Roll it away while there's no air in it, keeping a little tension on the sheet to ensure a neat roll, then come back up onto course again. No problems at all – and, of course, the same technique works for taking a few rolls to reef the sail.

Racing-foil headsails

These must really be bagged shortly after dropping. This is often inconvenient, particularly when short-handed and, it must be said, it makes them unsuitable for out-and-out cruising yachts. This doesn't mean you can't have a decent holiday aboard a cruiser-racer, but the foredeck is likely to be hard work.

Hanked-on sails

The traditional hanked-on sail is often seen 'stowed' in an unseamanlike bundle against the guardrails. To stow it neatly (as follows) is safer and should be a source of pride:

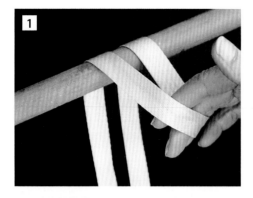

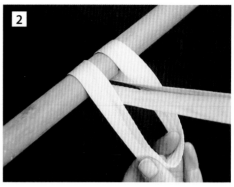

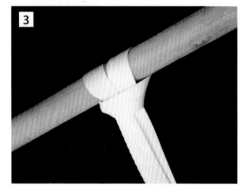

▶ The cow hitch is the best way of securing a sail tie to a guardrail in preparation for use.

- Attach a set of bungy or webbing sail ties to the top guardrail using cow hitches.

- Drop the sail and detach the halyard.

- Heave the clew right aft and hold it up against the top guardrail.

- This creates a bag along the foot into which the remainder of the sail can be rolled, always hauling the leech aft.

- When it's all in there, tighten the roll, then sweep the foot from outboard to inboard underneath the body of the stow and on over the top, to create a tube of smooth, crease-free sailcloth.

- A further refinement is to detach the tack before you bring the foot round. The tack can then follow the foot round the stow. When it's right round, reattach it to the forestay in a suitable place.

A headsail stowed like this cannot collect water if any washes over the foredeck, and it is therefore unlikely to be swept over the side in even the most extreme circumstances. It is also lifted clear of any weed or mud that comes aboard with a mooring or anchor.

▶ The sea state suggests that the wind is a steady force 4, and this day-sailer has one reef in the main, to give her skipper a safe, exhilarating day on the water.

● SAIL SELECTION AND SHORTENING DOWN

Most yachts are rigged so that they can carry full sail comfortably in winds of force 3–4, or 10–15 knots of breeze. As the wind strength rises, you'll find the boat heeling more than you'd like, her helm will become heavier and she will, in the end, grow hard to steer. It's self-evident that to ease the heeling, you must shorten sail. What's less obvious is why you are having to pull ever harder on the tiller to keep her going straight.

Helm balance

When a boat heels, two things upset the balance that keeps her helm light to handle. The first is that the sails have been offset to one side. If you were to attach a tow-rope half-way up the mast and pull the boat along while heeling her over, she would screw round. That's what's happening when you are sailing. Secondly, the hull itself becomes unbalanced as it leans. It is, in fact, no longer symmetrical and therefore tends to favour one side. Usually this is the same side as the rig, so the situation compounds and if you have a tiller you must heave it hard to windward to keep her on the rails. This state is called 'weather helm', even on a yacht with a wheel where you are having to steer to leeward; it is an integral part of sailing.

Because the mainsail is pulling from the aft end of the boat, it is forcing the stern to leeward and is therefore also exacerbating weather helm. If you are hit by a sudden gust and can't control the boat, letting the mainsheet off quickly ('dumping the sheet') will often bring her back into line. When the wind increases on a permanent basis, you must reef the mainsail.

The mainsheet traveller

Setting the mainsheet traveller can be a matter of considerable sophistication. As the wind strengthens, but before you reef (or reef again), you may find that when close-hauled or close reaching you can flatten the mainsail, and thus de-power it to some extent, by heaving down the mainsheet. The traveller is then employed instead of the sheet to alter the sail's angle to the wind. As you ease the sheet car to leeward, the helm should lighten up.

After hardening the mainsheet, the halyard may require some additional tension to balance the leading and trailing edges of the sail. Take up any slack on the kicking strap so that as you ease the sheet, the new leech tension and resulting flatter sail shape will be retained.

In light airs, with a fuller sail required to extract more power from what wind there is, try moving the traveller across to the centre, or even up to the windward side of the track, on a slightly eased sheet. Take it as far as you can without having the sail back-winded by the genoa, but never, never, allow the boom to weather of amidships.

In heavy weather, the traveller can be used with a flat, reefed sail to take out any tendency the boat has to 'gripe up' to windward, by easing the lower sheet block right down to leeward as far as it will go.

Choosing sails for the day

The right decision at the outset about what sails to set can make all the difference to a passage. Too much area and the trip will be fraught with drama. Too little and even if you don't die of boredom you might well miss a vital tide. If a boat offers

▶ The mainsheet traveller can do wonders for assisting mainsail trim, but if you are in doubt in the early stages when you've other things to think about, secure it in the middle.

a choice of headsails, only experience of her will tell you which to use, but for a typical 30-footer a good starting point might be:

- No1 – up to 10 knots (force 3)
- No2 – up to 14 knots (force 4)
- No3 – 14-20 knots (force 4-5)
- Storm jib in force 6 and upwards, if you really want to go out there at all.

Deciding how much roller sail to set is a matter of trial and error, always bearing in mind that the main and headsail should have more or less the same relationship to one another in terms of luff length that they had under full sail.

If the wind seems likely to exceed force 4, you'll definitely need a reef in the mainsail (see below). Put one in before you leave, if you can do so conveniently. If not, tuck it in as you hoist the sail.

Reefing the main

Years ago, reefing gear was often a lash-up of odd bits of rope and rarely-used rusty fittings. I recall my own first reefing experience when, book in one hand and heart in mouth, I struggled through the instructions. The literature was encouraging; 'Now you are snugly reefed,' it warbled, the pages whipping in the rising wind. My reef was unseamanlike and so shallow it seemed to make little difference. Small wonder I put off the next attempt until the cabin trunk* was almost in the water. Times have changed, thank goodness. Reefing gear today should be permanently rigged on most boats. It consists of the needful to pull and hold down the luff and the leech so that both are shortened in the right proportions to reduce sail area neatly. The sail has strong cringles* in its luff and leech to achieve this.

The luff cringle is either lashed down or, more likely, hooked to a 'ramshorn' at the forward end of the boom (the 'gooseneck'). The clew cringle is hauled down to the boom by means of a rope pennant* rove through a series of carefully sited blocks or sheaves either inside or outside the after part of the boom. The pennant not only pulls the cringle down, it also doubles as a new outhaul as it is snugged hard in.

Here is the procedure for reefing at sea:

- Steer on a close reach (15° to leeward of closehauled) so that the sail can flap when the sheet is eased. A close reach is chosen because this enables you to maintain control under headsail only while your crew reefs the main.
- Ease sheet and kicker, take up any slack on the topping lift.
- Ease away the halyard, pull down the luff and hook on the tack cringle, making sure you don't put a twist into the luff.
- Set up the halyard.
- Still on a close reach with the sail flapping, heave down the clew pennant (there may be a winch for this job) until the cringle is tight on the boom and positively

outhauled. There are a number of ways for making fast the pennant, but the most common is a jammer somewhere in its bight which releases the winch for the next reef. Where there is no winch, very likely you'll find a conventional cleat.

■ Ease the topping lift, pull the sheet in and set up the kicker.

■ There will now be a bag of sail hanging under the boom which you can choose to tie up out of the way. Except in extreme cases, it is not essential to do this, but if you are so minded, use sail ties to tidy up, passing them through the row of small

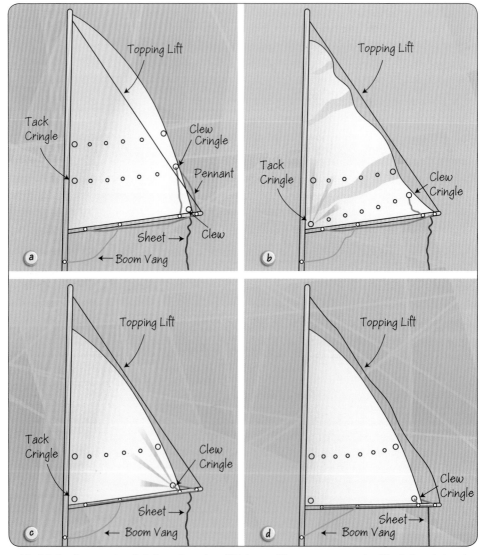

▶ Fig 5.1 Reefing a mainsail. A Ease sheet, let off kicker and heave up on topping lift. B Ease halyard, hook on reef tack cringle, then set up halyard again. C Crank down clew, with a winch if necessary. D Let off topping lift, set up kicker and let the sail draw.

brass eyelets running between the two cringles. If the sail is set in slides on the boom, pass the ties between the foot of the sail and the boom, particularly if they are of the type permanently attached to the sail known as 'reef points'. If, as is more usual, the sail runs in a groove, pass them round the boom as well.

- Pull down more reefs on top of this one as necessary. If you're caught by a sudden squall, it is acceptable to go straight for the second reef, but if you do there will be so much sail hanging under the boom that you'll certainly have to tie in the foot (Fig 5.1.)

Shaking out a reef

- Set up the topping lift before releasing kicker and sheet.

- Undo any foot ties first. This is important, because if you release the pennant without doing so, the small reef eyelets or the points will suddenly be taking a load for which they are not designed.

- Let off the clew pennant and overhaul any slack.

- Ease the halyard, unhook the tack, hoist away, then let off the topping lift.

- Check the luff tension, sheet in, set up the kicker and coil down the halyard.

● ENGINE TROUBLE-SHOOTING

So far in this book, we've been working on the assumption that the boat will be fitted with an inboard diesel. As years go by this has become the normal situation, but smaller yachts are still often powered by outboard petrol engines. While it would be comforting to imagine that our engines are mere backup for the sails, the facts of life for many of us mean that operating the boat without the engine would be, at least, a source of high stress levels. When an engine breaks down at sea, calling the AA is not an option, and while most ports have marine engineers, or 'get-you-going' operators, engine breakdowns are often so easily dealt with that it seems a shame to trouble these services. You can't handle a broken crank shaft on board, but such catastrophes are rare. Most breakdowns are far more mundane. Below is a list of common malfunctions that all skippers worthy of the name should take in their stride.

If hefting spanners and oily rags is absolutely not your bag, make sure there is someone aboard with a different point of view. It could make the difference between ten minutes rolling about at sea while you sort a minor problem, and a full lifeboat call-out.

Outboard engines

A petrol engine relies on electrics for ignition. It is therefore prone to spark failure at sea. Find out where vulnerable parts of the ignition system are sited so that you can dry them and/or spray them with a water-repellent such as WD40. Carry a spare set of spark plugs, have the engine serviced at least once a year and when it comes back, make sure that the whole electrical system from plug leads to covers looks as though somebody loves it.

So long as it has a spark, the only other thing an outboard needs is fuel. Locate the carburettor and practise a strip-down in the garage at home to make sure you know where the jets are. While you're at it, follow the fuel line from the tank to the filter and, if this is not of the 'clean-it-yourself' variety, make sure you carry a spare. A dirty fuel filter can stop an otherwise healthy outboard engine stone dead.

An even more popular source of trouble is water in the fuel making its way into the float bowl. This kills the engine every time. To fix it, all you do is remove the bowl, dry it out and pop it back on again. Make sure you can do this before you have to. Having carried out this pre-emptive maintenance, you'll also have discovered what tools you need and will have acquired any you do not have. Put a set on board and spray them with oil to rest easy while they wait for their moment.

Diesels

To start and run, a diesel asks only three things: electrical power at the starter motor, water for cooling and fuel at the injectors. Here are the problems that crop up commonly during normal operation, and what you can do to set them to rights:

Starter won't turn the engine over

■ Follow the heavy wires through from the battery and make sure all the terminals are clean and tight.

■ You may also find one or two lighter wires involved. Do the same for these.

■ If the engine battery really is flat and your battery switching system does not allow you to bring in your domestic supply in an emergency, dip into the tool locker, produce your jump leads and hook the two together ('+ to +', ' – to –'). If you haven't been over-privileged in your motoring career, you'll know what to do!

■ Keep a check on the tension and general condition of the belt that drives the alternator. If in the slightest doubt, replace it, or at least make sure there is a spare on board. It usually isn't hard to adjust the tension if you find it getting slack. The instruction manual will tell you how tight it should be, but if the book of words has taken a stroll you can safely set it up with about 15mm (⅝in) play in its longest run.

■ Designate an 'engine start battery', then guard and maintain it with your life. Never use it for any other purpose. Always charge it up every time the engine runs. Trickle-charge it every so often over a winter lay-up, and keep a regular eye on its electrolyte level. If it needs topping up more frequently than monthly, ask an electrician why, or scrap it. Check its voltage with a cheap meter (if the boat does not run to an in-built volt meter). If it goes down to less than 12 volts after a longish rest, or does not rapidly rise to 14 volts or a bit more soon after the engine starts, scrap it. It's only a small van battery and need not cost a lot to replace compared with the potential expense involved with an engine failure at sea.

Fuel

■ As with an outboard, pick a wet afternoon in harbour and explore your engine. Find the fuel filters and stock up on spares if there aren't any. The commonest reason for a diesel to stop, once it is running, is fuel blockage or contamination with air or water. A diesel cannot operate with air anywhere in its system, and if it has been struggling to pull fuel past a clogged filter, this can be the result.

■ If you suspect that fuel may be the problem, make sure you aren't out of diesel, then crack a bleed nut or screw on the injector pump. These are specifically installed to allow you to bleed unwanted air out of the fuel. The manual will indicate where they are, but if in doubt, try any hexagon on the face of the pump, carefully easing it off to see if fuel begins to flow. If bubbles appear, you definitely have a fuel problem. Follow the fuel line back past the lift pump (this supplies fuel from the tank to the high-pressure injector pump) and sooner or later you'll come to a filter with a replaceable element. Make sure there isn't a further filter on down the line somewhere, then dig out your spare element and change it. You may now have to bleed the whole system.

■ Many modern engines self-bleed. If yours is one of these, keep cranking on the starter motor after you've sorted out the filter and it will eventually start. Give the batteries a chance, however, and only crank it for six or seven seconds. Let the starter and batteries rest for half a minute before repeating the procedure. You can help a great deal by bleeding the filter, however, and if the engine is not self-bleeding you'll have to anyway. Slack off the bleed screw on the top of the

▶ A primary diesel filter – the first one you come to as you follow the pipe from the tank to the engine. This one usually clogs first if there is dirt in your diesel.

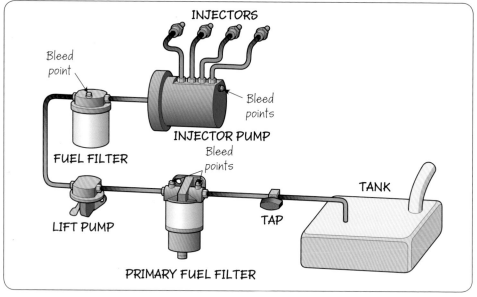

INJECTORS

Bleed point

Bleed points

INJECTOR PUMP

FUEL FILTER

Bleed points

TANK

LIFT PUMP

TAP

PRIMARY FUEL FILTER

▶ Fig 5.2 A diesel fuel system. On most units, the lift pump, filter and injector pump are attached to the main engine block. Follow the fuel pipe from the tank to identify all these important components before an emergency makes it necessary.

filter (if there is more than one filter, tackle the one nearest the tank first), then operate the manual pump handle on the side of the lift pump. Keep working this up and down until the bubbles stop and clean fuel runs out. Now nip up the screw and hit the starter.

If the engine doesn't self-bleed, carry out the process on the injector pump as well.

■ Many filters feature a glass bowl to allow inspection of the fuel. If you see water, open the plug at the bottom and drain it off. Where there is no glass bowl but there seems to be a drain plug, open it anyway and inspect what comes out. Let it run until you get clear fuel.

■ Make sure you have plenty of kitchen roll handy when you are bleeding a fuel system. A flexible plastic container of about a pint capacity can also prove handy.

Overheating

As reported in Chapter 1, the engine is cooled by circulating seawater, either directly, or indirectly via a heat exchanger. Whichever one it is, it will not affect the outcome of a blocked seawater system, the most likely source of over-heating. You can tell that the system is not circulating long before the over-heat buzzer goes off or the gauge registers 'boiling'. The sound of a marine diesel exhaust is muted by the waste cooling water injected into it. As soon as the supply dries up, the exhaust takes on a hollow, booming note that even a tone-deaf monkey could not miss. Furthermore, when the system is working properly the water can be seen pulsing out of the exhaust pipe. Check it as soon as you start the engine as a matter of habit. Often, if there is going to be a problem it happens straight away.

As soon as you recognise that all is not well, shut down the engine and deal with it. There are two main reasons why water circulation stops. Either the water filter has become blocked with weed, a plastic bag or other debris, or the pump has ceased to function. Here is your action list:

- Blocked intake filters are readily freed. On any properly built boat, a hefty filter will be sited close to the engine seacock. It may even be integral with it. It will be bronze or plastic, but in either case, the business of clearing it is obvious and straightforward.

- Shut off the seacock and open the filter. A small amount of water will escape into the bilge and you will see some sort of removable gauze bucket. Lift it out and with luck it will be full of horrors. Clean it up and replace it, turn on the cock and off you go.

▶ A typical Jabsco engine cooling water pump, with a spare impeller shown beside it. To replace the impeller, slacken off the six set screws, taking care not to drop any into the bilge, then remove the round covering plate, preserving the paper gasket if possible.

- If the filter is clear, leave it with its lid off and carefully open the seacock. If water flows in, there is no blockage to the supply. If it doesn't, make sure the cock is open, then poke a screwdriver down through it to dislodge the supermarket bag or misguided jellyfish clogging it up. Where the filter is fitted remotely from the seacock, you may have to remove the inlet pipe at the cock before poking around.

- If the filter and intake are both clear, but water does not circulate, the pump is generally the culprit. This works by means of a rubber impeller whizzing round in a flat cylindrical body. Follow the pipe from the seacock to find the pump. It is usually the first item you come to on the body of the engine itself.

- Shut off the seacock and carefully unscrew the face of the pump. Inside you will see the multi-lobed impeller. If this is obviously the problem, it will be missing a number of lobes. Withdraw it, install your spare, grease the ends of the lobes to help them round until the water arrives, and fire up the machinery. If the impeller looks OK, take it out for inspection anyway. Often, one or more lobes will have deteriorated sufficiently to reduce performance below a critical level.

- No spare? Sail in. Only call for help if there is some real danger other than the inconvenience of having to wait for a breeze – then expiate your infamy by making a massive donation to the lifeboat fund.

- If you have no spare gasket (the original almost always breaks up on removal of the end plate), make a new one from any paper of the right sort of gauge, greased with candle wax or some similar product. Wax the paper, lay it over the pump end plate on the cabin sole and gently tap all round the mating face with your hammer. This creates a perfect imprint of the gasket which you can now cut out with your sharp scissors. If there are no candles on board, I'm sorry for you. Dinner must be a dismal, neon-lit affair. You have no romance in your soul and are left with only the mechanic's friend, universal gasket goo. If you don't even have that, shame on you. Once again you must brass up for your favourite charity.

TOOLS

To keep a boat running independently on short daytime passages you ought to ship at least the following:

- A modest but appropriate socket set
- A spanner set, of appropriate size and quality
- Adjustable spanners, large, small and tiny
- Mole grips medium – you won't regret carrying the smallest pair you can find
- Medium hammer
- Screwdrivers, large, small and medium with various heads – slotted and cross-head. A cheap set of jeweller's screwdrivers are invaluable for electrical work (£10 maximum from all good boat jumbles)
- Hand drill or rechargeable electric drill, plus a set of sharp bits
- Hacksaws. Large and small, with spare blades
- Wood tools for wooden boats, including saw and chisels
- Pliers, large, and sharp-nosed electrical
- Electrical 'multi-meter' – a cheap one is fine
- Sharp scissors
- A wire coat hanger to twist into a custom-made hook, a probe and a hundred less foreseeable instant tools

If you're beginning to get the idea that your boat should be full of odd bits and pieces, rather like a decent garden shed, don't ever knock it. You're starting to think like a seaman with self-reliance as your watchword.

6

ESSENTIAL NAVIGATION THEORY

The purpose of this chapter is to furnish the essential theory to carry you through the hands-on practicalities of the next one. With both comfortably astern it will be safe to go to sea, so long as you understand that any passages made at this stage must be chosen to reflect your level of knowledge. In other words, if you do decide to sail away at the weekend without having digested the 'Advanced Navigation' chapter, take it easy.

● POSITION AND DISTANCE

Because the sea is essentially trackless, you cannot define where you are as you might on land by saying, 'I'm three miles west of the Red Lion on the A123'. Something more absolute is required. The universal answer is a cross reference given in latitude and longitude (lat/long), as shown in the illustration (Fig 6.1). There is,

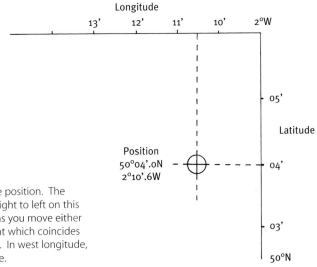

▶ Fig 6.1 A latitude and longitude position. The longitude scale increases from right to left on this chart. Longitude rises in value as you move either east or west from the 'zero' point which coincides with the Meridian of Greenwich. In west longitude, this can be confusing, so beware.

however, another method. Position can be read off as a distance and bearing (see below) from a known point such as a headland or a GPS Waypoint (Chapter 7). In practice, position is determined by means of a 'fix', which may be acquired by either traditional or electronic means, but more of this in the next chapter.

The fact that you can state where you are in different ways offers a free safety check. It is all too easy to make an error in reading the lat/long numbers from a GPS display. If you do the job both ways and the plotted positions coincide as they should, you can take it you've got it right. This concept of always looking for further sources of input or of checking one piece of data with another is one of the pillars of navigational thinking. You'll find it cropping up again and again.

Distance and the dividers

All chartwork depends on a few simple instruments. Longitude, latitude and hence distance in miles and decimals of a mile are transferred from the scales at the sides of the paper chart using dividers. The one-handed variety with the elegant brass curves are best. Not only do they look pretty, they can be used with your right hand while you hang on with your left. Hold them in your palm, squeeze the loop and they open. To close them again, bear in on the legs with your fourth and fifth fingers and the base of the thumb.

To measure the distance between two objects on the chart, place the dividers with one point on each. Now take them across to the latitude scale and see how many degrees or minutes they are showing. If the chart covers a number of degrees, choose a part of the scale nearest to your two objects, because the scale actually varies slightly as it moves north-south.

▶ Using dividers to measure distance between two points on the chart.

▶ Measuring miles off a latitude scale. Note that this one is running conveniently down the middle of the chart, a feature often found on privately produced charts and Admiralty Small Craft Folios.

DIRECTION

The compass

Direction at sea, and hence on the chart, is defined in 360° notation. Anything heading due North is 000°. Due South is 180°, West 270° and East is 090°. All compass bearings are referred to in three-figure convention in order to avoid any possible confusion. For example 090° is pronounced 'oh-nine-oh' to make sure nobody mistakes 'ninety' for 'nineteen'.

Inspect a chart to find a 'compass rose' showing the 360° of the circle. Once upon a time this was used to give the direction of any line on the chart such as a course or bearing. A course is read in the direction you are travelling, so that if you imagine yourself in the middle of the compass looking the way you are going, the bow of the boat will be seen over the correct heading (Fig 6.2 and Fig 6.3). The direction of an object you are seeing, on the other hand, is its bearing. This is taken once again with you perched on the compass needle and looking at the object over the top of the rose. The bearing is the number that lines up with the object.

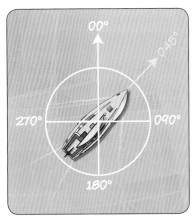

▶ Fig 6.2 Steering a course. The ship's head is looking towards 045° over the compass card. That is her heading.

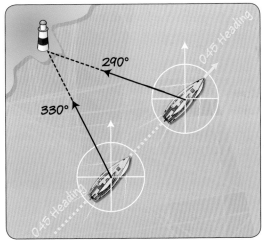

▶ Fig 6.3 When first observed, the lighthouse bears 330° on the yacht's compass. If she should change her heading at that point, the bearing of the lighthouse would not alter. As she moves her position, however, the bearing changes.

True and magnetic bearings and headings

Parallels of latitude sweep around the globe running exactly east-west and, as their name suggests, parallel with the Equator. The meridians of longitude are not actually parallel although they appear so on the Mercator charts we mostly use and can be taken to be so for small and medium-scale navigational purposes. In fact, they cut the Earth like slices of an orange from pole to pole and thus are lined up perfectly north and south. Unfortunately, the magnetic North Pole inconveniently fails to

▶ A typical steering compass. Course, '195 M'.

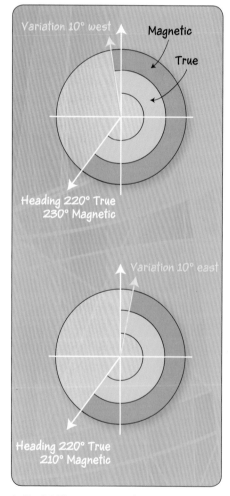

Variation 10° west Magnetic

True

Heading 220° True
230° Magnetic

Variation 10° east

Heading 220° True
210° Magnetic

▶ Fig 6.4 The compass and variation.

coincide with the geographic North Pole, which creates the anomaly called 'magnetic variation'. This throws the compass on your boat out by a significant amount. At the time of writing it is typically 4° or so to the west in Britain, but it varies throughout the world and with the years.

The extent of magnetic variation against the 'true', or geographic compass, is stated on the chart within the compass rose, leaving you with two choices. The first is to work largely in magnetic, setting up your chart protractor accordingly if it will do this, or using parallel rules (see below) if the chart has a magnetic compass rose. Unfortunately, some protractors are uncomfortable operating in magnetic and charts no longer universally have magnetic compass roses. Many people therefore prefer to convert magnetic compass bearings and headings to their true equivalents for chartwork. The modest skill required is well worth mastering. Once it's under your belt, you'll wonder why you ever hesitated.

The easiest way of making the true-magnetic switch is to remember that any compass with west variation will read greater than the true equivalent for a given bearing or heading. The diagram (Fig 6.4) will clarify this, but so long as you remember, Variation West, Compass Best, Variation East, Compass Least, you won't go wrong. For 'best', read 'biggest', and you have it.

Always denote a bearing or course with the suffix 'T' for true or 'M' for magnetic, then there can be no confusion.

If a heading is 100T, and there is 5° west variation, the heading on the compass is 105M ('variation west, compass best').

If the variation were 10° east, a compass bearing of 265M will be 275T (error east, compass least').

A further complication exists in some boats, where the boat herself causes the compass to deviate, but we'll deal with this in Chapter 12 on more advanced navigation.

Directional plotting tools

To use the compass rose, it is necessary to have a set of parallel rulers, one leg of which is held down on the plotted course line while the other is swung across to pass over the centre of the compass rose. The straight edge cuts the circle at the correct value of degrees. If the line in question is too far from the rose for the ruler to reach, the legs are walked across the chart, an awkward process which, on a yacht's small chart table, can be infuriatingly cumbersome. For this reason, parallel rulers have given way almost universally to the integral chart protractor.

A chart protractor incorporates a compass rose which can be swivelled around on a straight edge. To define a line, all that is needed is to orientate the protractor's rose north and south against the chart's lat/long grid, then rotate the straight edge until it coincides with the course or bearing required. As mentioned above, some protractors feature an offset in order to read in degrees 'magnetic'.

Plotting a course

To determine which way to steer from a departure point to a destination using a paper chart, first scribe a line along the edge of your protractor (with a 'soft', 2B pencil) from where you are to where you are going. Note whether the line

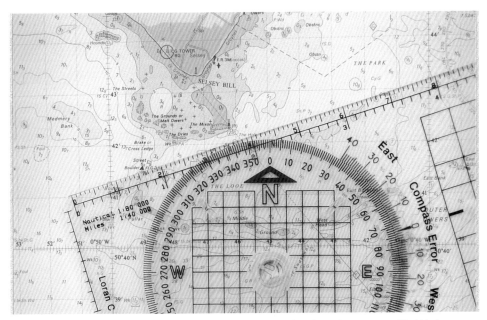

▶ Measuring courses and bearings. Lay the chart protractor's edge along the course and hold it there while swivelling the compass rose to line up with the chart grid, making sure that 'North' is to the top. Read off the course or bearing from the mark. In this case, it's between 072° and 073° 'True'.

passes too close to any dangers for comfort. If so, re-scribe it out of harm's way to another point you will be able to identify, either by means of some charted feature such as a buoy, or by fixing your position (see next chapter). Plot a second line from this point to your destination, always bearing in mind that once at sea you will certainly deviate to some extent from your ideal track. As you begin to build on experience, you may find you don't plot all your course lines, preferring to monitor your actual progress as the passage develops. Within limits defined by common sense, this can be an acceptable policy.

Once you have plotted a safe line to follow, read it off the protractor and correct it for magnetic variation. The result is the 'track'. This may also prove to be the actual course to steer, or it may prove no better than a starting point for adding in a number of other factors. If the destination is in sight you may decide not to steer by compass at all, but the line remains useful. When 'eyeballing' a passage, especially for the first time, it is vital not to make any false assumptions. The only way to be certain that what you really are seeing is what you think you are seeing, or would like to be seeing, is to double-check as follows:

> Work out from the chart what the course ought to be, steer in this direction, then look ahead and to the sides. Does what appears in 3-D add up to the chart's 2-D application? Are all the buoys and headlands exactly where you think they should be? If you have the slightest doubt, slow down and look again. Is it possible you aren't where you imagine you are? Make sure you haven't made a nonsense of the course by adding or subtracting 90°, or even 180°. This is a common mistake when orientating the chart protractor. Don't proceed, therefore, until you're absolutely sure everything looks right and is right.

Napoleon used to believe his opponents lost battles because they 'made pictures'. This was his way of saying that they forced things in the real world to look the way they wanted them to look in their minds. He, by contrast, observed things resolutely as they were and acted accordingly, even when he didn't like what he saw. The results stood him in excellent stead until he was finally let down at his Waterloo. His philosophy could be called the second law of navigation. The first, you'll recall, is, 'Always double-check data with as many sources as possible'.

'Never make pictures,' is a worthy companion for it.

● TIDES

Tidal heights

Tidal height calculations have a tendency to boggle minds. They baffled me for years until one day the truth dawned gloriously. Ever since, I have found them simplicity itself. The reason they have developed such a nasty reputation is that answers are required in varying situations, and students too often do not understand the nature of the question being asked. This is because they, like me all those years ago, have not taken the trouble to grasp the definitions. The secret of success in tidal calculation is to understand these. Even if you ultimately opt to devolve responsibility for crunching the numbers to a computer program or a calculator, the definitions remain axiomatic to deciding what it is you are trying to find out.

In Chapter 3, we learned the basic propositions about High Water, Low Water and secondary ports. We also defined the term 'tidal height'. If any of these are not crystal clear, recap them before you read on.

Now take a good, long look at the illustration (Fig 6.5). It probably appears rather alarming, so we're going to defuse it by taking each term separately.

Tidal height definitions

■ **Springs and Neaps** The terms 'spring' and 'neap' crop up a number of times in the tidal height diagram. They refer to large and small tides. The engine driving the tide is the gravitational pull of the moon, augmented by the sun. When the moon is full, or dark, it is lining up with the sun and the two gravities are additive, creating a large tide known as a 'spring'. At half moon, either waxing or waning, the pulls are subtractive, so the tide is much smaller, sometimes involving only half the volume of water of a spring. Such tides are known as 'neaps'.

The term 'spring tide' has nothing to do with the season. The name is incidental. Springs occur twice every month, at full moon and on the first showing of the new moon. At any stage in between, the tide is either growing

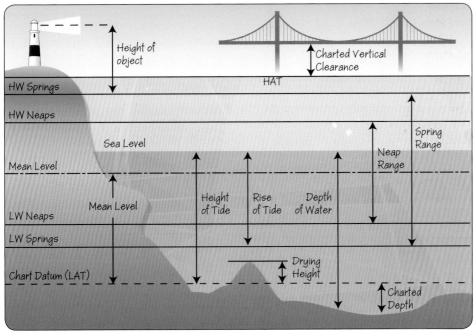

▶ Fig 6.5 Tidal definitions.

up towards springs or dropping back to neaps. Spotting which tides you are 'on' is easy. Just look up and down the heights in the tide tables and you can tell by inspecting the figures.

■ **Chart datum** as we saw in Chapter 3 is the Lowest Astronomical Tide (LAT).

■ **LW Springs and Neaps, HW Springs and Neaps** are all heights of tide above the base depth of chart datum. On any particular day, the height of High or Low Water may lie somewhere between the two.

■ **Sea level** is taken to be where the water is right now.

■ **Height of tide** is how far the water is now above chart datum.

■ **Rise of tide** is how far the water has risen above this tide's Low Water figure.

■ **Range of tide** is the full rise of a given tide between its High and Low Water figures.

■ **Depth of water** is what it says – the distance between sea level and the sea bottom – but in this context it is possible to be more specific. Often, calculating depth is the crunch, bringing a number of defined factors into play. The depth on this particular diagram is: Charted Depth + LW Springs + rise of tide. The fact that the Low Water figure is for spring tides is absolutely arbitrary and was selected for clarity on this particular diagram. On the day, it will be the Low Water for the tide in question.

Calculating heights between High and Low Water

The Rule of Twelfths

To work out how much tide is up at a given moment you must first remember that the Low Water height given for this particular tide will be there for the duration of the tide, until the next one takes over after twelve hours or so. This must be added to the rise of tide at the time required. Low Water is known from the tide tables, so the only item remaining is to work out the rise.

The easiest way to calculate the rise of tide in most areas of the world is to employ the universal rule of thumb, the 'Rule of Twelfths':

■ Determine the range of the tide by subtracting Low Water from High Water

■ Divide the range by 12

■ In the first hour of a standard six-hour tide, 1/12 will come up

■ The second hour will see an additional 2/12

■ The tide is really moving in its middle two hours. In both the third and fourth hours, 3/12 arrive

■ In the fifth hour things simmer down to 2/12 again

■ In the final hour, only 1/12 is left, and that comes in now

■ The same happens with a falling tide

■ The aide-memoire is '1,2,3,3,2,1'. Those are the Twelfths which rise or fall in the six hours. Clearly, if you require a rise at a half-hour time, you must interpolate the numbers. Fortunately these are generally pretty simple and the job can be dealt with by mental arithmetic. If in doubt, leave a substantial margin for error.

EXAMPLE:

What is the depth in Snug Harbour at 1030 this morning?
The charted depth is 0.8m.

From tide tables:

LW	0900	0.6m
HW	1500	4.2m

Tide range = 3.6m
1/12 of tide range = 3.6 ÷ 12 = 0.3
At 1000 1/12 will have risen = 0.3

In the second hour, 2/12 will rise, but we need only half this hour, so we'll take it as 1/12 = a further 0.3

Depth = CD + Low Water + rise (2/12)
Depth = 0.8m + 0.6m + 0.6m = 2.0m

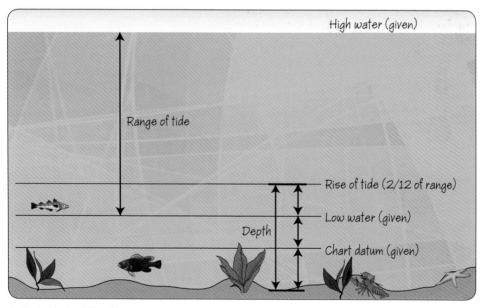

▶ Fig 6.6 Rule of Twelfths.

A final warning

The Rule of Twelfths only works perfectly in ports where the tide rises and falls with the regularity of a metronome. Many ports are not so well blessed. In the Solent, for example, the rule hardly works at all because of the famous double tides of Southampton. So if that is where you sail, you'll have to move straight on to Chapter 12 for the tidal section at least. In the West Country or Scotland, the rule is generally pretty reliable. The safe answer is to use it where appropriate, but don't treat it as gospel. The tide tables themselves are only predictions, and their absolute accuracy may be affected by strong winds or extremes of barometric pressure.

The bottom line is: always leave a fair margin for error, and if you decide to make a passage before completely sorting out the question of mid-tide depth calculations (see Chapter 12), choose a destination where this won't be an issue.

Secondary ports

So far, we have dealt with the question of secondary ports by grabbing a copy of the local tide tables. The question of how to handle secondary ports with the almanac will be considered in Chapter 12. By then, you may well have been using the techniques described above and should have the foundations of the business firmly under your hat. On the basis of 'one thing at a time', the matter should therefore present no special problems.

Tidal streams

In parts of Britain, tidal streams are so significant that they are more important to the passage-making yacht than a fair wind. In general, the tide reverses every six hours, but the change, or turn of the tide does not always coincide with local High or Low Water. You can be fairly sure that this will happen in a river, with the flood running up to the top of the tide and the ebb draining out until Low Water. Along the coast, however, this is often not the case. To discover what is going on out there, you must refer to the tidal stream atlas.

Tidal stream atlases

The Admiralty publish atlases to cover most of the coastline, but it is not necessary for you to go to the expense of buying one if you already have an almanac. Each one is reproduced here within a few pages of its reference port in small, but usable format.

Timing

Each diagram represents an hour of tide referred to a local standard port. The time is given as '3 hours before HW Dover', etc. This means that at exactly that time (don't forget to correct for BST if necessary), the tide will be behaving as shown. Although the change in rates and directions really happen differentially, they are taken conventionally to run as shown for a whole hour. This hour commences 30 minutes before the time stated and ends 30 minutes after, thus straddling the moment in time when the data are strictly correct. It does NOT start at 3 hours before HW and continue until 2 hours before.

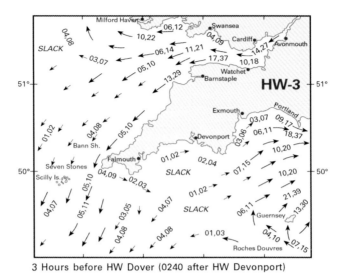

▶ Fig 6.7 A tidal stream diagram. Extract reproduced from the **Reeds Nautical Almanac**.

Information

This particular tidal stream diagram (Fig 6.7) shows a schematic chart of the west of England. Note the arrows, indicating the direction of the stream at various points, and also the numbers giving the rate. Immediately south of Swansea, these read '17, 37', the neap and spring rates respectively. They are multiplied by 10 to do away with the distraction of the decimal point. Thus, the streams at this place will be 1.7 knots at neaps and 3.7 knots at springs.

At any time between springs and neaps, you must interpolate. If you're untalented at mental arithmetic, you'd better buy a copy of the Admiralty Tidal Stream Atlas for your local area, because inside the front cover is a well-explained diagram for dealing with this accurately. If, like me, your brain is happy working out darts scores and the change from a round of drinks, it's surprising how well you can do the sum in your head. Inspect the tide tables and assess how today's range relates to springs and neaps, then apply this in your head to the range difference between the two. The answer might not get you 100% in a written yachtmaster paper but it won't be far wrong, and the method has served many a working sailor all his life.

EXAMPLE

Spring rate	2.5 knots	Spring range	6 metres
Neap rate	1.2 knots	Neap range	3 metres
Rate difference	1.3 knots	Range difference	3 metres

Today's range 4 metres = neaps + 1/3

Rate is:

1.3 knots (neaps) + 0.4 knots (approximation of 1.3 x 1/3) = **1.6 knots**

Some tidal generalities

■ **Progress** is critically affected by the tide. If a boat is beating to windward and making good 3 knots, a fair tide might easily raise this to 5 or 6, whereas a foul tide can leave her sailing on the spot. A yacht beating with a fair tide of more than a couple of knots generally makes better progress than one reaching against it.

■ **Depth** In a river or even along the sea shore, the shallower the water, the slower the current. If the tide is fair, stay out in deep water, but if you're punching a foul stream, do all you safely can to creep into the shallows.

■ **Tide rips** often occur near headlands or in narrow tidal channels. Look out for these on the chart, where they are likely to be denoted by symbolic ripples or whirlpools. They can generate rough and sometimes dangerous water, especially with a strong wind against the tide. Expect the tide to run more strongly off headlands, and read your pilot book (Chapter 8) for details.

■ **Wind against tide** invariably creates a rougher sea than when the stream is running to leeward. Be ready for this, and watch out for the situation being exacerbated by tide rips, or shoals over which you may have decided to sail.

● THE ELECTRONIC CHART PLOTTER – A CAVEAT

Using an electronic chart plotter makes many of the tasks in this chapter much easier. It may even deal fully with issues of tide. However, before you can get the best from a plotter it is important that you understand which questions to ask it and are confident you can cope if it goes down. Learning to navigate without one remains, therefore, far more than a formality. We'll take a closer look at using a plotter responsibly in Chapter 12, on Advanced Navigation.

TIME ZONE (UT) For Summer Time add ONE hour in non-shaded areas	FALMOUTH LAT 50°09'N LONG 5°03'W TIMES AND HEIGHTS OF HIGH AND LOW WATERS	Dates in red are SPRINGS Dates in blue are NEAPS YEAR 2009

JANUARY		FEBRUARY		MARCH		APRIL	
Time m	Time m	Time m	Time m	Time m	Time m	Time m	Time m
1 0155 1.5 0748 5.0 TH 1420 1.5 2010 4.7	**16** 0302 0.9 0854 5.3 F 1527 1.0 2119 4.9	**1** 0242 1.3 0836 4.9 SU 1505 1.3 2056 4.7	**16** 0335 1.5 0912 4.7 M 1554 1.6 ◑ 2129 4.5	**1** 0152 0.9 0745 5.1 SU 1412 1.0 1959 5.0	**16** 0231 1.1 0804 4.9 M 1446 1.3 2016 4.9	**1** 0248 1.3 0850 4.7 W 1511 1.5 2105 4.7	**16** 0259 1.7 0843 4.3 TH 1509 2.0 2100 4.4
2 0227 1.5 0821 4.9 F 1453 1.5 2044 4.6	**17** 0338 1.3 0930 5.0 SA 1604 1.4 2153 4.7	**2** 0318 1.5 0915 4.8 M 1544 1.5 ◑ 2140 4.6	**17** 0410 1.8 0948 4.4 TU 1632 2.0 2213 4.3	**2** 0223 1.0 0818 5.0 M 1444 1.2 2033 4.9	**17** 0258 1.5 0832 4.6 TU 1511 1.6 2047 4.6	**2** 0338 1.5 0946 4.4 TH 1606 1.8 ◑ 2208 4.5	**17** 0344 2.0 0935 4.0 F 1604 2.2 ◑ 2155 4.2
3 0302 1.6 0859 4.8 SA 1531 1.5 2126 4.5	**18** 0416 1.5 1006 4.7 SU 1643 1.7 ◑ 2231 4.4	**3** 0403 1.6 1008 4.6 TU 1636 1.8 2242 4.4	**18** 0501 2.2 1041 4.0 W 1732 2.3 2323 4.1	**3** 0258 1.3 0857 4.8 TU 1521 1.5 2117 4.7	**18** 0328 1.8 0908 4.3 W 1542 2.0 ◑ 2129 4.3	**3** 0449 1.9 1106 4.1 F 1730 2.1 2339 4.3	**18** 0501 2.2 1047 3.9 SA 1734 2.4 2315 4.1
4 0344 1.7 0944 4.7 SU 1618 1.7 ◑ 2217 4.4	**19** 0500 1.9 1047 4.4 M 1730 2.0 2324 4.3	**4** 0507 1.9 1121 4.3 W 1752 2.0	**19** 0617 2.4 1218 3.9 TH 1854 2.5	**4** 0343 1.5 0949 4.5 W 1611 1.8 ◑ 2218 4.4	**19** 0415 2.2 1000 4.0 TH 1642 2.4 2230 4.1	**4** 0635 2.0 1248 4.1 SA 1919 2.0	**19** 0622 2.2 1238 3.9 SU 1855 2.3

▶ Tide table extract from **Reeds Nautical Almanac**.

7

PRACTICAL NAVIGATION

One of the things that put me off wanting to learn about navigation was that there seemed so much of it. The good news is that you don't need it all at once. For much of the time you will be merely 'eyeballing'.

On any given day, you are unlikely to be asked to deploy every navigation skill in the Day Skipper syllabus. The art lies in deciding what is demanded by a specific situation. So long as you have prepared a passage carefully, you should know what this is, which in turn minimises the time spent at the chart table at sea. The essentials must be covered, of course, but skippers with their heads crammed semi-permanently into the navigation system are not doing the job properly. Rocks are not inside the GPS receiver, neither are boats bent on colliding with you, but either might well be right ahead, so your priority is to deal with navigation as smartly as possible, hop back on deck, see what's going on and reassure the crew that you're in charge.

Navigation breaks conveniently into two sections. 'Where am I', and 'Where do I go from here'. We've taken a preliminary look at the second question in Chapter 6. When you're out at sea, the first issue becomes vital.

● KNOWING WHERE YOU ARE

The essence of navigation – our first law – is to draw conclusions only when information from at least two sources has been duly sifted. We have an extremely accurate and reliable source of position fixing in GPS (Global Positioning System), and it is tempting to hand over all responsibility to it. Unfortunately, this can prove unsafe.

In Shakespeare's version of Julius Caesar's demise, Cassius observes shrewdly that, 'the fault, dear Brutus, is not in our stars, but in ourselves'. He never said a truer word. The most common source of GPS error has nothing to do with the satellites that drive the system, nor even in a loss of volts from on-board batteries. It lurks in our own human capacity for screwing up. Any computer, including GPS, is only as good as the data it is given. If you misread one of the many decimal places it offers, or poke your dividers into the wrong latitude mark on the chart, you will plot a position as spurious as if you had used a compass bearing 15° adrift. Punch in the wrong waypoint co-ordinates and your whole day can turn to rats in short order. Add to this the spectres of electrical failure or even, heaven forbid, Uncle Sam – who at present maintains the satellites – deciding to take the day off, and you will see that you owe yourself an extra check.

The foundation of the navigator's philosophy of ongoing back-up is the 'estimated position'.

Estimating the position

It is a good idea to plot a position on the chart at least every hour while on a daytime passage, and more often if common sense demands. The first action to achieve this is to note how far you have come from your last known position, and in which direction.

Distance measurement is carried out by means of a 'log'. This can be either a through-hull device reading out via an electronic instrument or, occasionally, a rotating impeller towed astern racking up the miles on an analogue dial. Logs are usually fairly accurate, but when they start promising precision to two decimal places of a mile, remember that this means 20 yards, not always realistic in a rough sea. The log measures only distance run and, perhaps, speed 'through the water'. A boat sailing in a current is carried across the seabed by the water in which she herself is moving, so the distance she makes through it will not be the same as distance made good 'over the ground'.

Direction is taken from the course actually steered, duly corrected for any extraneous factors. These are dealt with more thoroughly in Chapter 12. For the time being, you must either skip ahead or accept that your estimated positions (EPs) may lack pin-point accuracy.

The dead reckoning position (DR) is worked up from the last known position by plotting a course line in the direction you have travelled, measuring distance run using the latitude scale and the dividers, then transferring it to the line. Scribe a small cross onto the line with your pencil and that is the DR, the starting point for all estimated positions (Fig 7.1).

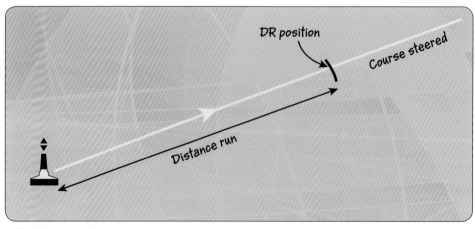

▶ Fig 7.1 Dead reckoning.

Tidal effects and the reality of speed

Tide may have a significant input into an accurate EP. Cross-sets will be dealt with in Chapter 12, but on many coastal passages, the stream runs along the coast just as you are doing, and is therefore directly either for you or against you. If this is the case, the DR is best adjusted for tide before plotting. A run through the water of 6 miles by log in a fair stream of 2.5 knots becomes a plotted run of 8.5 miles over the ground. It's worth noting the contrast that with the same tide running foul, the yacht would make good a mere 3.5 miles.

This concept of the boat moving through water, which is itself moving over the ground, is an important one. Don't forget that while the log reads water speed and distance, any speed given out by a GPS must be 'over the ground', so don't join the foolish who boast in the bar that their 35-foot yacht was doing 10 knots that afternoon. 'Hooey!' is all I have to say to them. 'Over the ground with fair tide' maybe but, lightweight racing yachts and occasional downwind blasts under spinnaker apart, no sailing boat ever exceeded the speed dictated by the limiting factor of her length. Just for the record, this is something in the order of 1.35 x √LWL (waterline length). The answer comes out in knots. Work yours out for yourself.

Plotting ahead

Once you have a position on the chart confirmed by a fix, always lay your protractor along the course line to see where it will take you in the near future. Some teachers insist on students plotting ahead with a pencil line. There's much to be said for this, except that a sailing boat rarely ends up following the exact track her skipper has optimistically planned. Many people find it natural merely to lay the protractor on the chart and inspect the anticipated track visually. Myself, I'm content to leave whether or not to plot ahead formally to the skipper's good sense, but it must be taken care of one way or the other if you're to stay out of trouble.

Once you have a realistic estimate of where you might be, you must take steps to confirm it. Very often, there isn't a pressing demand for super-accuracy. If you are sailing in waters where no dangers threaten and you can eyeball your position by reference to an identifiable buoy close at hand, that is really all you need do. When an exact position is required and no navigation aid is conveniently placed to make life easy, you should fix your position more formally.

The fix and GPS

A position line (PL) is a line plotted on the chart from a known object to the boat. It carries a single arrowhead at the end away from the object to show what it is. Typically, the line is defined by a magnetic bearing. If the boat is on one PL when a second is taken and plotted, she must also be on the new PL and can therefore only be at their intersection. This is the old definition of a fix in the Admiralty Manual of Navigation. It hasn't changed throughout history and, even with GPS, it still holds good.

GPS works by sensing signals from a 'cage' of satellites orbiting Earth. Their position is known at any given second, and the receiver derives a series of electronic

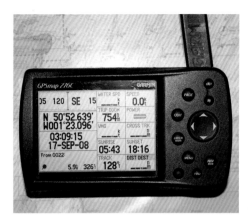

▶ A main screen readout from a hand-held GPS unit. Note the clear lat/long position, the 'Track' (course over ground, or COG), and the accurate time. The various other boxes can be fine-tuned by the user to read out more or less whatever he or she may fancy

position lines from them, inspects the intersection and hands you the results as a lat/long fix.

GPS is now our primary fixing system. It is accurate to a boat's length; so accurate in fact that if you don't treat it properly, it may appear to be more precise than the chart itself. Transferring its fix to a paper chart is easy, but you must double-check each plot (see also 'waypoints'), because this is where many mistakes are made.

With an electronic plotter, any errors transferring data to the chart go away, but it's still vital to double-check against depth (see below) and 'look out of the window' to make sure that all is more or less as you expect.

Chart datum

Like any other survey, a chart must be drawn with reference to some datum point. This has nothing to do with the 'Chart Datum' of lowest astronomical tide. Over the years, different nations have adhered to varying systems, or 'datums', for determining absolute latitude and longitude. This never mattered a hoot until GPS came along, because nobody could tell the difference. Now that we have such aspirations of precision, however, these matters have assumed considerable importance.

The default datum for most GPS sets is 'WGS84', an international datum designed to cope with this situation. If your receiver is working on this datum, it may well give out a position that appears 100 yards or more adrift when used in conjunction with a British Admiralty chart. Many of these are still drawn to 'OSGB35'.

You don't need worry about the deeper technicalities of all this, but you ought to search your GPS manual to see whether the receiver can be set to different datums. Many can. Now inspect each working chart in the vicinity of its title. You'll find all manner of information, including a note about 'satellite-derived positions' which states the datum. If you can bring your set into line, do it. It will only be a matter of pressing a couple of buttons. If not, the chart also explains how to adjust a GPS position derived from WGS84.

If you are using an electronic chart plotter, the question of datum ought to be managed by the software, which means you have to do nothing with it. However, this does not always work out as one might like and certain areas away from home waters have been notorious for what are known as 'datum shifts'. These mean that the GPS places the boat to its own datum and the electronic chart is working to a different one. If you see your boat sailing up the beach on the screen when she is really in deep water, this may well be what is happening. The bottom line is clear. Don't rely slavishly on a plotter, useful though it undoubtedly is. Cross-check by eyeball and keep your wits about you, especially in fog. Don't get too bogged down worrying about such considerations. Most of the time they are pretty esoteric, and much of your inshore navigation is going to be eyeball pilotage anyway, but in dense fog you'll be delighted to know how to bring your GPS up to its full potential.

Other sources of fix

Although GPS is by far the most accurate and convenient source of fix, there are still occasions when some alternative other than a hand-held back-up set becomes pertinent. One day in the 1990s, the whole GPS system was shut down by its operators. It can happen again, and Sod's Law states that it will be just as you're negotiating an awkward passage into a strange harbour.

A good cut and a cocked hat

Grand old terms, these. And they describe important concepts. The 'angle of cut' is the angle at which two or more PLs intersect. The closer this comes to 90°, the less will be the linear error created by an inaccuracy in one or other bearing (Fig 7.2). Anything much less than 40° or so is undesirable if there is any choice.

The 'cocked hat' is the small triangle (or at least, you hope it's small) created on the chart at the intersection of three PLs (Fig 7.3). The purpose of the third PL is to

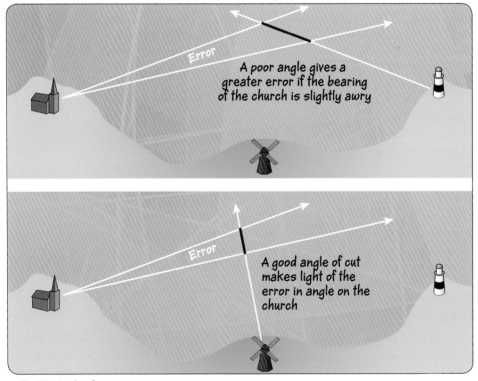

Error

A poor angle gives a greater error if the bearing of the church is slightly awry

Error

A good angle of cut makes light of the error in angle on the church

▶ Fig 7.2 Angle of cut.

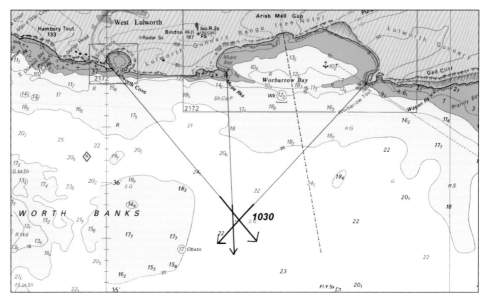

▶ Fig 7.3 A traditional three-point fix worked up from handbearing compass position lines to form a 'cocked hat'. Note that the objects chosen give a good 'cut' as shown by the almost equilateral triangle.

cross-check the other two. The three almost never cross exactly, and the size of the cocked hat becomes a standard by which the quality of the fix may be judged. Select your objects to create a neat, equilateral cocked hat if you can.

It is perfectly acceptable to take bearings from objects on either side of the yacht, but beware of the almost diametrically opposed pair, which make a poor cutting angle and are of very little use.

Sources of PL

▪ The bearing of an object taken with a handbearing compass – this requires practice in a rolling boat, so get some in. Shore objects are best, as buoys may drift a little.

▪ Be creative when looking for bearings. Don't just use lighthouses and beacons. Try a chimney or two, the edge of an island, or anything else you can dream up.

▪ The best PL of all is a transit. Line up any two convenient charted objects and you have a bomb-proof PL of great accuracy. Remember to check it with your compass to make sure you've identified the correct objects. If the transit is an

SKIPPER'S TIP   RECORDING FIXES

Any fix, whether by GPS or other means, is noted on the chart and marked with the time it was taken. This allows it to be cross-referenced to the vital navigation log book.

officially set-up leading line (Chapter 8), so much the better, and don't forget the old trick of lining up two headlands just as they 'open' or 'close'.

- If a charted object is coming into line with the ship's head, steer to bring it dead ahead or dead astern and use the steering compass to take an easy bearing. An object that may be brought abeam can be sighted along the mainsheet traveller. When it is 'on', note the course, then add or subtract 90° to find the bearing.

Depth – a third arbiter

At this stage, we can be fairly confident of our position. We have an EP confirmed by the fix. But the good navigator is always on the lookout for further corroboration. Depth can often supply this. It is the work of seconds to note the sounder reading immediately after taking the bearings or the GPS reading for a fix. So long as the depth stands up, you have further verification that all is well. If it doesn't, you'd better take another look at the GPS readout, or maybe that third bearing that you weren't so sure about…

Sometimes when you are busy, there won't be time to work up a proper estimated position (EP), so you will merely 'guesstimate' where you are in the light of distance run, tide and course. You'll then plot the GPS fix, make sure it ties in with your unplotted estimate and call it a day. In some circumstances this is acceptable practice, but if you take the liberty, make absolutely sure to bang in a depth sounding for an empirical second opinion.

The log book

A position, whether fix or EP, has two functions. The first is to tell where you are now. The second is the basis for onward navigation. Assuming the boat is under way, any fix has passed into history even before it is plotted, but if you noted the log reading when it was actually taken, you can refer back to it to begin a new EP at any time. A log book doesn't need to be a pre-packaged, complex record of everything from the course steered through the tidal conditions and leeway to the state of the skipper's marriage. It can be a cheap exercise book with a few simple columns you've ruled yourself. This is what mine looks like:

Time	Log	Course	Weather	Remarks	Engine
1035	26.4	135M	SW4 – cloudy	Sticky End N cardinal buoy abeam 1M to stbd. GPS fix on chart	Off

Some navigators log the lat/long of each GPS fix on the basis that if they plot it wrongly, they can always go back and double-check it. There is good sense in this, particularly on a long night offshore when people are tired, but it is also acceptable to plot the fix straight from the screen to the chart, so long as you make sure it coincides with your cross-references then enter it into the log book with time and log reading.

Logging on the plot

If conditions are bad and you're trying to minimise time spent at the chart table, there is no reason why you should not dispense with the log book on a short passage, pencilling all vital information on the chart instead. It may not be the approved system for a formal Day Skipper shorebased course, but many sound American yachtsmen do it as an accepted policy, so it can't be totally heretical. Write down the time and log reading alongside a buoy on the chart as you pass it for real; give plotted fixes a log reading as well as the time; a course to steer might have its number written along it, and so on. The crucial thing to remember is that the purpose of the log book is to give enough information to back-track to the last known position. If you elect not to use the book, you must be able to secure this information from your chart jottings.

● ONWARD NAVIGATION

We've seen how to plot the track you want to follow, starting from a known position and using the chart protractor to determine a course. The GPS can take care of this by using its waypoint facility. It will even tell you how far you have to go, but it can neither think for itself nor read the chart, so the important safety aspect remains up to you.

Waypoints

A waypoint is a position of significance towards which a navigation computer such as GPS can direct the ship. Its precise situation may well be arbitrary, so it's up to you where you put it. I generally site a safe waypoint near my destination and, if the passage involves course changes round headlands or obstacles, I put further ones at the places I would ideally like to be when I alter course. When a waypoint is at a buoy with deep water all round it, there is no harm in making the exact location of the buoy the waypoint. In such cases, dividers and pencil aren't nearly as accurate as the position you may find in an almanac or published waypoint list. If the waypoint is off a headland, it's a bad idea to use the official location of a lighthouse, because that will take you onto the rocks. The practical answer is to choose a convenient point close to seaward – perhaps outside any tidal disturbance – then measure its lat/long with protractor and dividers. If you are using an electronic chart, siting a waypoint is as easy as clicking the mouse.

Using waypoints safely

To work a waypoint, first decide what its position is going to be, then enter it into your GPS. I'm not going to be drawn into the mechanics of this, because it's like the old saying, 'different ships, different long splices'. Read the manual, punch in the numbers and practise the process until it is second nature, because you may occasionally demand a new waypoint in a hurry. Most receivers allow you to name a waypoint. If not, give it an unambiguous number and note down immediately what it is.

Next, if you haven't already done so, carefully plot the waypoint on the chart, and double-check both this and the lat/long you have fed into the GPS. I can't over-stress that this is the source of the majority of GPS-induced navigational blunders. The conventional symbol for a waypoint is a vertical cross enclosed by a square (see page 98).

When the time is appropriate, hit the 'go to' button, or whatever is required to activate the waypoint. The GPS readout will give you a bearing and a distance to it. Lay the plotter across the waypoint on the chart with the angle set at this bearing. You will immediately see if the course is safe to steer. If so, go for it. If it is dubious, shape up to clear the obstacle, then hit 'go to' again and reassess the situation. In waters that are anything other than clear of all dangers and obstructions, it is critical that you repeat this process as frequently as prudence dictates. It only takes a few seconds and could save your ship. Tides or even leeway can drift you steadily away from the safe track originally envisaged. The GPS's job is to keep giving a new course to steer to the waypoint. It won't know if the heading takes you right across the yacht club lawn.

The waypoint as a plotting check
Since plotting from GPS is a proven source of casual error, it is satisfying to use a double-checked waypoint as a handy control. Plot the lat/long fix, then re-plot the position as defined by the distance and bearing given from the waypoint. The two should coincide exactly. If not, find out which is wrong. It might even be the waypoint itself (Fig 7.4).

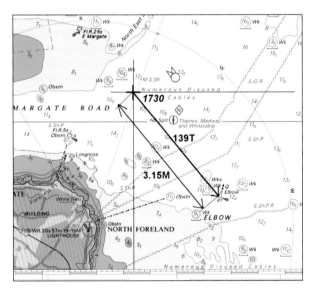

▶ Fig 7.4 Cross-checking a charted GPS fix. This fix has been plotted as a lat/long position, then confirmed by noting its range and bearing from Elbow buoy, which has been entered as a waypoint.

This sort of mental discipline at the chart table is a classic example of the time-honoured principle of two sources being better than one. It also shows how GPS can make a good navigator better. The lazy pilot who never confirms anything but relies implicitly on a single unverified electronic readout is even more likely to come unstuck than he was in the bad old days.

Using basic GPS to combat drift

We'll be dealing fully with tidal cross-sets in Chapter 12. Also the 'cross-track error' function of GPS. You are more than ready to go sailing now, however, so when you're out there, bear in mind the following and don't be too ambitious.

If the bearing of a waypoint towards which you are steering steadily alters in the same direction, you are in a cross-current. As likely as not, what you are seeing on deck with your own eyes will confirm this. If eyeball observation doesn't clarify which way you are being set, use the protractor to create a visual aid. Starting with the original bearing then rotating it to the present one should make the situation obvious. Try steering 'into' the drift by 15° or so. If the bearing steadies, stick with the new heading. If not, adjust again, and so on.

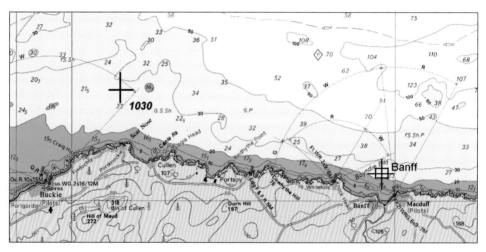

▶ Fig 7.5 A passage from Buckie towards Banff and MacDuff. Note the waypoint 'Banff' plotted a mile outside the harbour entrance to keep the route and landfall clear of dangers – you'll eyeball in from here in any case. Note also the GPS fix at 1030. This will have been checked by log reading and course steered, then further confirmed by depth sounding.

Passage planning

The secret of a successful passage lies in up-front planning. When I was running Day Skipper practical courses regularly, I always spent half an hour on the first evening talking about this subject. It was time well spent. A plan shouldn't take more than an hour to compile. Once you are into the swing of things, 10 or 15 minutes will often cover it, but do it you must. At its most basic, I wouldn't think of setting out from my own berth in the Beaulieu River on a five-mile hop to Cowes without noting what the tide will be doing, both out-bound and coming back. Here is a list of items to consider:

- **Charts and distances.** Have you a passage chart as well as another with enough detail for entering harbour? Can you make the trip in a single tide, etc?

- **Pilot books.** Refer to these where appropriate (Chapter 8).

- **Tidal streams.** Vital in waters where currents run hard. Pencil in the day's real-time hours in tidal stream diagrams. It's easier to relate to '1530', than '3 hours before HW Portsmouth'.

- **Tidal heights.** If these are critical, work them out in advance. You won't fancy the job later if you're bouncing along heeled over.

- **Weather.** Goes without saying, but what about tomorrow? Will you be faced with a hard beat home when all hands are hung over?

- **Dangers and obstacles.** These should include any shipping lanes you might want to avoid. Don't be paranoid about ships. If their channels are empty and you want to use the water, go ahead. Just be aware of the complications that may arise if a lane proves busy when you arrive.

- **Essential strategy.** Decide which way you will go and where you will make your major turns.

- **Pilotage plan.** Familiarise yourself with what you expect in the way of close-in pilotage at your destination – see Chapter 8 for details.

▶ Planning a passage concentrates the mind, but it can be fun as well.

8

ARRIVING IN PORT

Making a passage between ports is all very well, but any experienced sailor will tell you that arriving and leaving provide the main sources of stress. We've dealt with departing, but what happens when you turn up in a strange port? Where do you go? Who do you ask for a berth? What are the likely regulations and who gives out the parking tickets? These are the sort of questions that once preyed heavily on my own mind. After all, nobody wants to look like an idiot, but before berthing and its attendant issues hit the top of the priority list, the boat must be worked safely into harbour, so we'll begin this chapter by considering one or two of the close-in navigation techniques that come under the heading of 'pilotage'.

● PILOTAGE

Pilotage is really the visual navigation demanded by circumstances where orthodox chart or GPS work are inappropriate. You'll sometimes handle whole passages in easy waters using pilotage techniques only, but whatever the nature of the journey between harbours, you will certainly be 'piloting' when you enter port. Situations here can develop rapidly and your proper place is on deck for decision-making. Besides, any plot you might manage to lay down will be out of date as soon as it is made. Monitoring progress across a plotter screen can be very reassuring, but it is critical that you master a few seat-of-the-pants techniques. These are used in addition to keeping on the planned side of any buoys and recognising sea or landmarks from the chart, because there are still times when your own eyes can outgun technology. Besides,

▶ Two pairs of eyes are always better than one. Involve your crew when piloting.

you might simply prefer to use a paper chart, or the volts might drain down an electronic hole.

The safe line

From time to time you'll require a safe track through dangers which may be out of sight below the water. This need not be so alarming as it sounds. Pre-plot a safe line through them on the chart, then determine some way of visually defining it. The most common ways of achieving this are set out below, and you'll note that GPS is not amongst them. 'Cross-track error' (Chapter 12) between accurately plotted waypoints is theoretically capable of delivering the goods, but it can be confusing to peer into a screen when instant course alterations may be required, especially when you aren't doing it every day. Furthermore, your pencil, dividers and even the lat/long scales on your chart may not be sharp enough or detailed enough to work up the waypoints to the required degree of pinpoint precision. GPS is not your 'Number 1 tool' in pilotage. It's better to do the whole job by eye where you can.

A safe line can be defined in various ways:

SKIPPER'S TIP | **THE SINGLE OBJECT**

Simply steering towards one object which, to begin with, appears to be a safe guide, can prove dangerous. Because you are not on wheels rolling down dry tarmac, cross currents or even being blown sideways can set you off your desired track. If you are aiming for a single marker and not checking your track in any other way, you may not realise this is happening until it is too late.

Transit of two leading marks

This is truly the pilot's friend. As we have seen, the transit offers the best of all worlds. Unambiguous, clearly defined and easy to see. Harbour authorities sometimes set up special transits called 'leading marks' that can clearly be observed from seaward. These are charted and mentioned in pilot books. Use them whenever you can, but don't forget to double-check them with the handbearing compass to ensure you are looking at the right thing.

Unofficial transits

Where no set-up transit exists, you can often find your own. Lay the protractor on the chart with the edge more or less on the required line. Now inspect the chart along the plotter's edge, ahead or astern of where you will be. As likely as not you'll find two objects which, with a minor but safe alteration from the ideal track, can be brought into line. It doesn't

▶ A classic 'unofficial transit' of an old and new lighthouse coming into line.

▶ The inshore rock in line with the distant headland sets up a fine 'unofficial' transit. If both items appear on the chart, as these probably will, the transit can be used for formal navigation as well as a means of checking sideways drift.

matter whether they are ahead or astern. Either will do. This powerful technique for keeping out of trouble improves with chart-reading practice and is well worth spending time on.

Compass bearing

Never as good as a transit, a safe line can often only be defined by noting the bearing of a readily identified object ahead or astern. If it is ahead, steer towards it and keep noting your heading. If it alters, steer to compensate and bring the object back to where it should be.

Where the object is astern, you must run what is known as a 'back bearing'. Have a crew member observe the object over the handbearing compass as you steer away on a course which must be the reciprocal* (± 180°) of the bearing. Initially, the object

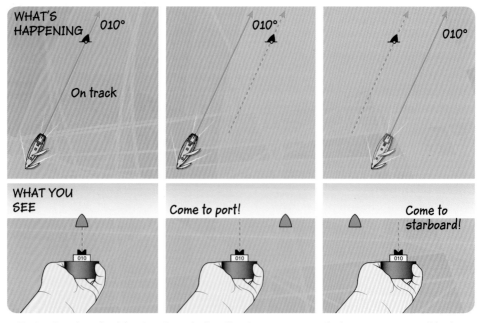

▶ Fig 8.1 Running a back bearing. Keep the handbearing compass on the bearing you want. If the boat drifts from her track, your action will be immediately obvious.

should be in the sights of the compass. Keep looking down the correct bearing. If it drifts to one side, it is easy to determine what correction is required. Don't take changing bearings on the object as it drifts then try to translate these into course alterations. You'll be faced with a brain-twister to sort out which way to turn (Fig 8.1).

The clearing line

Sometimes, danger lies on one side of a line only, so a full-on 'safe line' is not required. In such cases, it is only necessary to pre-plot a line on the chart which defines the limits of safe navigation, more or less parallel to your track. So long as you don't cross it, you're OK. This is called a 'clearing line', and is defined by the same means as the safe track, ie the transit is favoured, a compass bearing might do, etc (Fig 8.2 and 8.3).

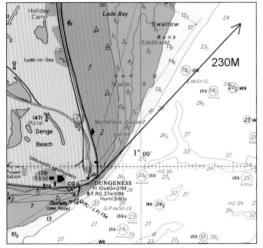

▶ Fig 8.2 A clearing bearing. A yacht coming from the northeast and wishing to round this headland close inshore will need some means of defining the position of the shoals north of the point. So long as the compass bearing indicates a lower value than 230, the yacht is over the line and standing into danger.

▶ Fig 8.3 Safe line pilotage. The route through the rocks into this harbour in western Ireland is defined by three safe lines. The first (upper left) is a bearing on a beacon. The second and third are marked by transits. The most difficult part of entering a harbour like this for the first time is often identifying the marks. Once they are recognised, it's plain sailing. All bearings noted on a chart are given as 'True, from seaward'.

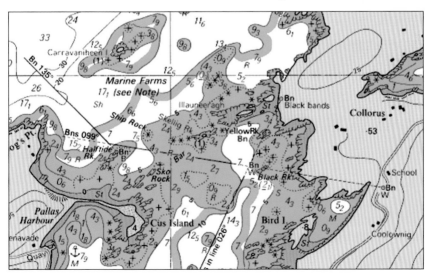

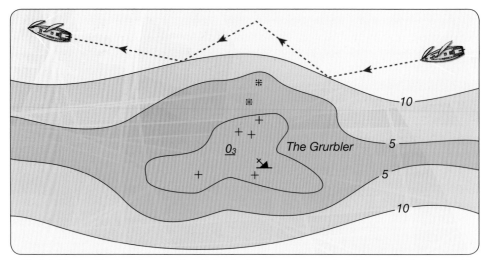

▶ **Fig 8.4** Clearing line by echo sounding. Using the 10m contour as an invisible clearing line keeps this yacht off the Grurbler Shoal and associated rocks.

The echo sounder

The sounder can sometimes supply an additional factor in determining where you are for day-to-day pilotage – when you are too close to the edge of a river, for example. If you look more deeply into this apparently obvious statement, you'll realise the sounder is actually providing a clearing line. The procedure can occasionally be brought into play when circumstances are less blatant (Fig 8.4).

The pilotage plan

Passage planning was an important sub-heading in the previous chapter. It is equally vital at the pilotage stage. To go swanning into a harbour you have never entered before without preparation is asking for trouble.

SKIPPER'S TIP   **PILOT BOOKS**

Books such as my own *Shell Channel Pilot* for both sides of the English Channel remove much of the sting from preparing pilotage tactics. Experienced people, often with local knowledge, have put these works together. Their harbour plans indicate useful lines of approach, and they advise the best marks to use, complete with tips for finding the difficult ones. All manner of further information is given, as diverse as ferry movements, unexpected cross-sets and useful landmarks. Some even advise whether the marina has a laundry. Pilot books can enrich your visit with social and historical details. While much of the essential information may also be found in a good almanac, the pilot book is far more detailed.

As an instructor, I have learned that people's minds work in different ways and nowhere is this more obvious than in the pilotage plan. Some write everything down, others draw a complete plan of the harbour, noting courses and distances between objects. I myself use the chart, if this is of large enough scale, jotting down vital bearings and distances, ringing important buoys and generally clarifying in advance anything I will not be able to plot in the heat of the moment. I suggest you experiment, devising your own system for a plan that tells you everything you need to know as you work up from the sea to your berth. Be thorough at the outset. In due course, experience will show what can safely be left out.

CHOOSING A BERTH

If the destination is an open roadstead, you'll be anchoring. In a more sheltered harbour, there will often be more choices. As well as lying to your own ground tackle, there could be moorings, a tidal wall, or you might pay top dollar for the comfort of the local marina. Decision factors will include cost, privacy, security from the weather and the convenience of accessing shore facilities.

Anchoring
See chapter 14 for how to set about this.

There is absolutely no reason why you should not anchor overnight in a safe place. Long-term cruisers spend years safely lying to their own gear. Often, this has the advantage of being free of charge, although shamefully this is not the case in many areas of southern and southwest England. The chosen anchorage must have the following qualities:

Shelter This is required from the wind and, more particularly, the waves. If an anchorage is open in one direction, you must be sure the wind and sea will not come in from there, or be prepared to shift berth if they do.

Deep water Adequate depth is needed to float the boat at low water. Chapter 12 includes the mechanism for working this out.

Landing You will want some means of landing from the dinghy unless, of course, you are happy to stay on board. In the absence of a smart pontoon, a beach is fine so long as you don't mind wet feet and carrying the small boat up to the High Water mark.

▶ Choosing a berth in an anchorage is a skill that comes with experience.

Moorings

The same factors apply as to anchoring. However, you must also consider whose mooring it is.

Visitors' moorings These are usually clearly marked and are often operated by the harbour authority. Help yourself. Payment is generally collected by the harbour staff who turn up just as you are about to have breakfast. Occasionally you are obliged to go ashore and declare yourself to the harbourmaster. The pilot book should tell you which, but if the buoys are the property of a yacht club it will usually be the latter. Nip up to the club house, buy a pint if the bar's open, and ask the steward.

Private moorings It is an unwritten convention that in the absence of designated moorings, a visitor can pick up any suitable buoy at his own risk, having due regard to the size of the boat and the likely nature of the mooring itself. The understanding is that if the owner returns, the visitor must shift berth immediately. If you have moored under these circumstances, it may therefore prove bad manners to leave the boat unattended if she is to be out of sight for any length of time.

Should the owner of a mooring be 'bolshie', he is out of order, so long as you are pleasant in manner and available to move your boat.

Tidal walls

The pilot book will tell you whether this is the place to go or not. If it is, be careful that there is enough water to float you at Low Water. Drying out against a wall is not part of the Day Skipper syllabus, but if you do find yourself with no option, remember that the greatest danger is that of the boat falling over, so secure a halyard ashore and keep it set up as the boat goes down. When she touches, crank it up to give her a 5° list inwards and that should do. If in doubt, shift anchors and water carriers to the side decks next to the wall. Check your fenders at all times until the boat has settled.

Marinas

It is good practice to call the marina ten minutes or so before arriving. VHF is the preferred method (see the pilot book or almanac for the numbers), but if you have no licence, you might feel more legal using the mobile phone. The berthing master will ask for the boat's length and the probable duration of your stay before directing you to a suitable berth. He may tell you 'which side to' and, if he doesn't, it is in order to ask so as to avoid last-minute scuffles around the deck. If you need assistance with your lines there is no shame in asking. Any decent marina staff would far rather help you out than have to sweep up chunks of fibreglass.

Once the boat is secure, stroll up to the office and make yourself known. Settle up and enquire about keys or security numbers for the showers and marina gates. Where there is no means of contacting the staff in advance, the pilot book may tell you which are the visitors' berths. Help yourself, then go and find the berthing master. Accept any request to shift berth with good grace. Should all else fail, hang off any free berth, preferably an outside one, walk up to the office and enquire. If they've gone home, settle in until morning, but be ready to move if the berth-holder comes back at midnight.

9

ETIQUETTE

All of us make naïve errors in behaviour when setting forth on a venture with unfamiliar conventions. I hope the next page or two will save you from the worst of them. Some consider these nuances of decorum outdated and unimportant, but they speak volumes about you to anyone who really knows.

● FLAG ETIQUETTE

Ensigns

Your ensign will be red or blue. Red is the proud flag of the British merchant fleet and can be worn by any merchant or private vessel. The blue is for Naval officers and those with an Admiralty warrant, for which a charge is made. You can apply for a warrant if you're a member of a yacht club that enjoys this special privilege (usually a 'royal' club), in which case the blue is only flown when the member is on board and his or her club burgee flying. From time to time you'll also see 'defaced' ensigns of both persuasions. These generally carry the arms of a club. The white ensign (St George's flag with union colours in the corner) is the ensign of the Royal Navy. The only yachts flying it are those whose owners are members of the Royal Yacht Squadron.

Ensigns are flown always from the taffrail* unless the yacht is gaff-rigged, when it may be flown at sea from the peak of the gaff*. A ketch or yawl at sea may fly hers from the mizzen* masthead.

Never fly a Union flag or any form of EU 'ensign'. Both are illegal.

Burgees

These are small triangular flags denoting your yacht club. Traditionally they are flown from a short stick at the masthead where they double as wind indicators. This looks good and is eminently practical, unless you have a veritable forest of antennae up there. If so, you must contrive a very long stick (an elegant and classy solution) or settle for the compromise of a burgee flown from a signal halyard to the spreaders.

There is no longer a convention regarding lowering burgees with ensigns, and many honest operators keep theirs up round the clock. My old mate Robert, however, who had done his time under a proper professional yacht skipper, always lowered ours with the ensign. Robert would also turn out at 0800 sharp to raise colours, no matter how foul the weather or gruesome his hangover. I have tried to follow his example.

Times to fly your colours

In good King Charles' days, when thrifty Pepys was running the Navy Board, one of his underlings spotted that large sums were spent annually on replacing bunting. It was therefore decided to have HM ships strike their ensigns when darkness meant they would not be seen anyway. The bunting bill was cut in half and the policy passed into folklore. Any yacht worthy of the name still carries on this tradition, although many owners have clearly never been let into the secret.

▶ It's 0800 – time to raise the colours.

You're obliged to fly a national ensign at sea in coastal waters and when entering or leaving harbour. It is also customary to display it when berthed, so long as you are in commission (ie, if you're on board and not laid up). When not under way, colours should be hoisted at 0800 Local Time (0900 in winter) and brought in at sunset or 2100, whichever is earlier.

● RAFTING UP

'Rafting up' means securing alongside another yacht. This involves close human proximity and, like all social events, has developed its own standards of behaviour.

The hail

This is the first phase of the raft-up. Don't try to raft when there is some other berth reasonably convenient. Where there is no choice, it's best to select a boat either the same size as, or bigger than yours, then pass slowly by and ask her crew if they mind you mooring alongside. Should nobody be on deck, hail her positively by name and hope someone appears. If nobody shows up, go ahead anyway.

People generally prefer it if strangers don't raft up to them. This is understandable and you must do all you can to reassure them you know what you're about and won't indulge in drunken revelling at 0230.

A canny response to your hail along the lines of, 'We're leaving at 0500,' is the hoariest chestnut in the book. The old hand produces one of two diplomatic responses:

1 'So are we.'

Or . . .

2 'We quite understand. We'll be up to let you out, then we'll re-berth and hop back in the bunk for an hour or two.'

The former might even be true if there is a critical tide you are both looking for. The latter calls the host's bluff. The chances are he will mysteriously change his mind and you'll find him still there when you surface at 0800 for colours. If he really does leave, so be it. You'll wake when he starts his engine. With luck it'll be fine and you'll enjoy crawling back into the bunk after doing the honest thing by the neighbours.

Securing alongside

When you raft up to another boat, the fendering between you is your responsibility. If a new boat arrives and hangs off you, it's hers, and so on.

Never toss a tangle of rope to the crew of another boat and assume they'll drag you in. The practice can enrage. I've known otherwise decent people misfield the whole 'bunch of bunglies' on purpose, allowing it to fall in the water, rather than bust their own backs doing somebody else's work. This, however, is a counsel of despair. My wife adopts a kinder solution. She makes the ends fast and leaves the new arrivals to do the pulling. I recommend this as the best policy from both sides, so when you're coming in, hand the other crew enough rope, ask them to secure the end, heave in the slack yourself and make the bights fast on board as though arriving at a dock.

If nobody answers your hail, creep aboard quietly in case they're asleep, then make fast with bow line, stern line and springs.

Whatever happens on your initial approach, as soon as you are secure alongside, take a bow and a stern line ashore if this is at all feasible, so that your boat carries her own weight.

Crossing another yacht's deck

A yacht is like a sounding box. Anything you tweak or stamp on will reverberate, scoring you nil points in the social fourth division, and to jump from a dock onto someone else's deck (or your own for that matter) is the nadir of bad behaviour. When there is someone on deck, always ask, 'Mind if I come across?'. Nobody but a seasick gorilla with a personality problem has ever been known to refuse, but it sets out your stall as a caring person and helps the day along.

Always cross another yacht forward of her mast. Using the cockpit invades the only excuse for a bit of privacy a rafted-up yachtsman can hope for. The reason is that it's almost impossible for human nature to resist taking a discreet peep down the companionway where you may be embarrassed to witness anything from the family at their corn flakes to acts of depravity that boggle the sheltered mind.

If you have to swing up from the dock using other people's shrouds, concentrate on not 'pinging' them as you let them go, especially at closing time when the neighbours are turned in.

Never put your boot heel down on someone else's deck. Always walk on the balls of your feet, placing the side part down carefully first. I learned this technique as a ten-year-old in the Wolf Cubs. Using it, I can get from my boat to the dock, all 15 stone of me, and the neighbours don't know I've been there, except for the additional list from my weight.

Late-night parties

These seem to happen to me all the time and they need careful handling if you are not to be justly branded the worst kind of villain. There are two answers:

1 Some neighbours look like funsters, so invite them along. You'll enjoy meeting them and they might bring a decent bottle.

Or . . .

2 When this is clearly unsuitable, make sure you go below decks at around pub closing time, even if it's a glorious summer night. Once inside with the hatches battened down you can carry on and most of your racket will be contained. At least you've shown respect. Caterwauling in the cockpit until dawn will justly earn you the hate of the harbour.

If in doubt, imagine what your actions would make you think were the situation reversed, then apply the test of Leviticus and 'love thy neighbour as thyself'. It's not always easy, but it works wonders in a raft-up.

▶ A raft-up can be a satisfying way of bringing friends together or, if handled badly, a nightmare of inconsiderate behaviour.

10

WEATHER

Any good skipper takes the liveliest interest in the weather. For a short daytime passage, what is happening now is the first item on the agenda. If you don't fancy the look of what's on offer, don't go out. And don't be swayed over-much by what others are doing. Only experience will tell you what you and your boat are comfortable with.

Closehauled sailing really is the crunch for the cruising yacht. It's all very well for old salts like me to pontificate that a 32ft yacht ought to be able to work to windward in force 7, but you might decide that you don't like beating in force 5, and I for one wouldn't blame you. A heavy thrash upwind can be good fun for an hour or two in sheltered water, but after half a day in the open, I generally find myself considering the alternative advantages of tiddlywinks. So don't over-reach yourself. Confidence will come, so long as you aren't timid about advancing your expertise.

Having made an assessment of current conditions, the next job is to consider the forecast, bearing in mind that if you're away from home overnight, you have to get home again, or even move on. The main thing to avoid is ending up at the wrong end of a stiff wind with no time left for contingency plans. Reading the forecast is the only answer, but before looking into where to find the best ones, we need to establish what the terms used actually mean.

● THE BEAUFORT WIND SCALE

Despite the creeping tendency to describe wind strength in knots, miles per hour and even, Heaven help us, kilometres per second, Admiral Beaufort's 19th century system remains the most useful for a small sailing boat. It was created in response to a naval requirement for some universal measurement. The sea state is described in detail because this is the visible effect of wind. The scale thus enables an observer who, like me, chooses to have no wind instruments, to judge the probable wind strength visually.

The original Beaufort scale described how much canvas a 'wooden walls' frigate could carry closehauled as the wind rose. Later versions advised smacksmen whether or not to house their topmasts. Mine may prove more useful to the Day Skipper. The sail plan suggested is for guidance only. Boats vary considerably when it comes to sail-carrying power. So do crews.

Beaufort Scale

BEAUFORT NUMBER	KNOTS OF WIND	NAME	SEA SATE	SAIL PLAN FOR A CLOSEHAULED 28FT YACHT
0	←····1	Calm	Sea like a mirror	Crew in pub, or motoring
1	1–3	Light air	Ripples with the appearance of scales are formed but without foam crests	Very probably motoring with mainsail sheeted in
2	4–6	Light breeze	Small wavelets, still short but more pronounced. Crests have a glassy appearance and do not break	Full main and genoa
3	7 – 10	Gentle breeze	Large wavelets. Crests begin to break. Foam of glassy appearance. Perhaps scattered white horses	Full genoa, maybe one reef in main
4	11 – 14	Moderate breeze	Moderate waves, taking a more pronounced long form; many white horses are formed. (Chance of some spray)	Full or 2 rolls in genoa, one reef in main
5	17 – 21	Fresh breeze	Large waves begin to form; the white foam crests are more extensive everywhere. (Probably some spray)	2–4 rolls in genoa 1–2 reefs in main
6	22 – 27	Strong breeze	Sea heaps up and white foam from breaking waves begins to be blown in streaks along the direction of the wind	Genoa rolled in as far as it will set properly. Main deep-reefed
7	28 – 33	Near gale	Moderately high waves of greater length; edges of crests begin to break into spindrift. The foam is blown in well-marked streaks along the direction of the wind	Storm jib Deep-reefed main/trysail. Motorsailing with flat main/no jib
8	34–40	Gale	High waves. Dense streaks of foam along the direction of the wind. Crests of waves begin to topple, tumble and roll over. Spray may affect visibility	Survival. Storm jib and trysail/deep-reefed main, or motorsailing with flat main/no jib

You'll be able to work out for yourself that force 6 is as much as any normal person wants to see and that, really, force 5 or less is optimum, with force 3–4 as emphatically 'what the doctor ordered'. If you even sniff forces 7 or 8 in the forecast, you do not want to be there at this stage of your development. I have left everything above this (the full scale reads up to 12 – Hurricane Force) because it should be seen as irrelevant for our purposes.

You can safely add one force to your 'comfort zone' for downwind sailing, but always remember the issue of wind awareness. The apparent wind feels a lot less than the true wind when you are running, a phenomenon that has led to many a nasty shock.

▶ The sun may be shining, but it always pays to look over your shoulder. The sky to windward here looks as though the skipper should be tucking in a reef in good time.

VISIBILITY

You'll hear visibility given out in weather forecasts. The following terms need to be understood:

Good more than 5 miles
Moderate 2–5 miles
Poor 1000 metres – 2 miles
Fog or very poor visibility Less than 1000 metres (can be as little as 25 metres)

This means that on a good day, you'll be able to see your destination as soon as this becomes geographically possible. In moderate 'viz', things may appear misty in the distance, so fixing other than by GPS could be tricky if you are out at sea. When the visibility is poor, unless the waters are easy to navigate or you know them well enough to be able to identify an object such as a headland as it looms up, you might consider waiting for an improvement. With fog forecast, think very hard and read Chapter 13 before going to sea, even if you do have GPS.

WEATHER SYSTEMS

Weather in Britain is dominated by two types of system: high pressure and low (Fig 10.1). Both form circulating bodies of air and certain types of weather are generally associated with them. The RYA have prudently left the details of this for more advanced courses, but I have set out the essentials below, because I believe they will help you understand the yacht's barometer and make more sense of the marine forecasts.

High pressure

A 'high' is a large, stable system that often hangs around for a while, especially in summer. Air circulates clockwise around it in the northern hemisphere (the other way down south). It generally brings fair weather. In its centre there may be little or no wind other than local sea breezes. At the ends of the year, visibility may be less than ideal under a 'high', while in the warmer months it can allow early morning fog to develop along coasts and in rivers. Such mists often 'burn off' with the rising sun.

Low pressure

'Lows', or 'depressions', are more vigorous than highs. Winds blow anti-clockwise around them (clockwise in the southern hemisphere) and they often bring strong breezes and rain. Typically in Britain, a low will track north of you, funnelling winds across your area from a westerly quadrant. It may also carry frontal systems where different air masses mix and where the worst of the weather is found. Here's what you experience as a low passes north of you. The whole process takes a day or so on average.

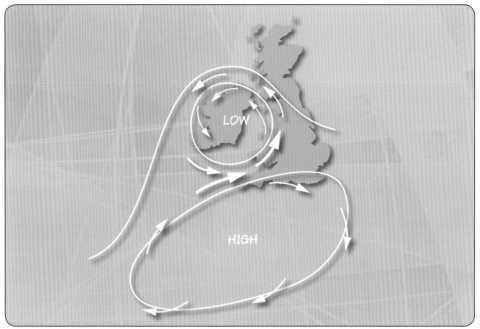

▶ **Fig 10.1** Air circulation around high and low pressure systems. Note the accelerated wind where the systems 'squeeze' together.

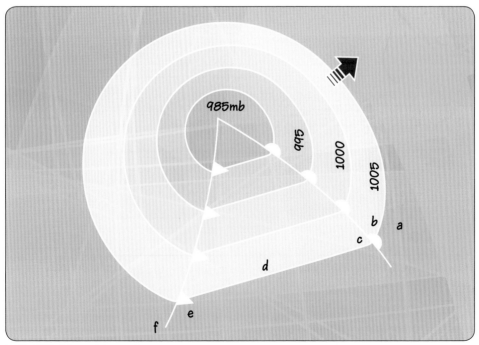

▶ **Fig 10.2** A frontal depression.

Explanation of the development of a depression (Fig 10.2)

a The wind backs (shifts anticlockwise) into the southwest, south or southeast as high cirrus (pronounced 'sirrus') cloud and 'mares' tails' spread over the sky from the west. The barometer begins to fall.

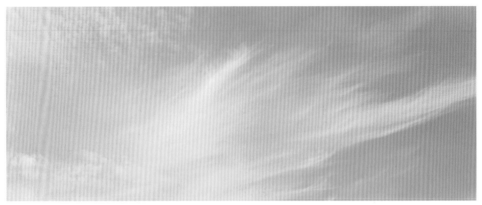

▶ Mare's tails. Often the unwelcome precursor of a warm front and bad weather.

b The wind stiffens and cloud cover comes lower. As the warm front approaches, visibility may deteriorate for a time.

c Rain begins, light at first, then heavier as the front passes. The clouds are now lowering and grey. The wind may well veer (shift clockwise) as the barometer steadies out and visibility improves somewhat.

d Between the fronts, rain will be intermittent and the wind most likely southwesterly. The barometer will be fairly constant and low.

e Cold front time: heavy rain, rising glass, wind veering.

f After the cold front passes, the weather will improve, with showers, perhaps heavy and squally for a time, and good visibility. Clouds often pile high into the blue sky looking like 'ice-cream castles', sometimes with anvil-shaped tops as the wind veers.

▶ A huge cumulonimbus cloud of the type associated with the passage of a cold front. There will be heavy showers and hard gusts for a while, but there's at least a hope of better weather soon.

In the centre of a low

If a low passes clean over you, the wind won't know what to do and you will find the seas as confused as you are. It doesn't happen often, but when it does, you'll probably be thoroughly soaked and you certainly can't rely on the wind. You might experience very little breeze, followed shortly by a great deal, so watch out if the forecast says, 'cyclonic variable'.

● SOURCES OF WEATHER FORECASTS

Wherever I am pulling in a forecast from, I always make a note of parts relevant to me as it is given. If I don't, I invariably forget the details. Get into the discipline of taking this trouble and you won't be sorry.

The shipping forecast

Beleaguered by pressure from programmers, a few unsung heroes at BBC Radio 4 have kept this world-class show on the road. The shipping forecast is broadcast at specific times which vary with the whims of the powers-that-be (see your current almanac) and gives information for all the sea areas around Britain's coasts. Check the map to find your area, and listen to the adjacent ones as well. If the weather is coming in from the west as it often does, it's well worth knowing what's going on out there, because this may affect you tomorrow. The land forecast that follows the early evening shipping bulletin can help cast light onto its mysteries.

Inshore waters forecast

Attached to the shipping forecast at the most antisocial times (very early morning or small hours), this is the one you really want. It divides the coast into useful tracts and gives an invaluable 48-hour outlook. If you're bamboozled by all the headlands and weather stations, check that vital almanac. They're all in there.

Shore radio stations

With VHF, you can listen in to Cullercoats or Portpatrick radios, which repeat the shipping forecast at designated times. Details may vary and are found in the almanac.

Local radio

BBC local radio stations often broadcast the relevant sections of the shipping forecast. Those in popular sailing areas such as Radio Solent also give 'sailing forecasts'. 'Solent' has a daily slot, sensibly timed to coincide with most people's breakfast, that is habit-forming listening aboard every yacht from Selsey Bill to Portland.

Navtex

This is a dedicated radio receiver that prints out all sorts of useful material including weather forecasts and gale warnings. If your boat happens to have a receiver, so much the better.

SKIPPER'S TIP   **PRESS AND TV**

General forecasts can give a useful overview of the developing picture. Weather is always rolling on, even if we're taking little notice, and it's far easier to make a good decision if you don't arrive at today's weather from a standing start. So keep an eye on the TV and the papers in the days leading up to a cruise.

▶ Fig 10.3 Sea area map.

Internet

If you carry a computer on board, there are now many places where there is a good chance of hooking up to the Internet. A typical example is the sort of 'pay up front on-line' WiFi system offered by many marinas. Often, a number of marinas sign up with the same provider, which means you can part with your cash while lying in one, then enjoy using the rest of the money you've invested at their sister outfits. If you don't fancy marinas much, mobile phones and datacards are becoming ever more useful for connecting to cyberspace.

Once you're connected with broadband, the sky's the limit for weather forecasting. Try www.metoffice.gov.uk and www.xcweather.co.uk for starters.

The marina office

Today's marinas almost always publish some sort of daily weather forecast. Usually this is downloaded from the Internet, complete with maps. There should be a three-day prognosis as well details of the delights in store for today.

You meet some very nice people discussing their chances as they hang around posted met reports. Many a lifelong friendship has been struck up while commiserating about the horrors on offer from the Clerk of the Weather. It's only a short hop from the bulletin board to the snug bar of the Scuppered Sailor where skippers rapidly become specialists in making the best of a bad job.

11

MAKING THE PASSAGE

● PREPARATION

I am writing this on the day before Good Friday. I keep my boat in the West Solent and plan to spend Easter weekend sailing locally with my family. For the past couple of days, I have been glancing at the tide tables and monitoring weather trends. I know the waters and the options I have for destinations, and have reached certain conclusions. It looks like Chichester, especially if the promised northerly wind kicks in. In short, I've been passage planning, informally, in the privacy of my own head. By the time I arrive at the boat tomorrow evening, all I'll have to do is to double-check my charts and decide what time to get under way on Saturday morning. I've also been planning the victualling with my wife. How many meals will we eat aboard? Do we want cooked breakfasts (you bet we do, and it's black pudding for me)? What about drinks? Will we have the chance to go shopping when we arrive at Itchenor (the pilot book seems to suggest not)? Is it going to be cold? Do we need to take woolly vests and stock up on coal for our stove? And how much diesel do I have left after the winter?

Much of this material never appears in 'official' passage planning lists, yet it is often the guts of a happy result. Take time to think through every aspect of a proposed trip, not just the navigational nitty-gritty.

Engine

Running out of engine fuel is as bad a mistake as failing to verify the level in the gin bottle. Make sure you have plenty, plus any other consumable fluids such as lube oil, stern-tube grease, ionised battery water, even antifreeze if the cooling system needs occasional topping up. While you're thinking about engines, make sure you have a spare water-pump impeller, a fuel filter element and an alternator drive belt.

Fresh water

This is technically domestic victualling, but because water lives in tanks, I tend to consider it as part of the deck crew's responsibility and fill up while I'm topping off diesel at the fuelling berth. Running out of water is not life-threatening on a daytime passage, but it's the sort of nuisance that saps morale and leaves nothing to drink but the beer. Since the long-established and popular practice of a little modest drinking while sailing is now frowned upon by a caring legislation, law-abiding skippers might find themselves arriving thirsty in port.

Victualling and cooking

Decide whether or not your at-sea eating will be more ambitious than grabbing a choc bar and a mug of tea. Once in harbour, you can hash up anything the galley is good for, but on passage things are different. Even experienced hands can feel sick if called on to rustle up a hot meal while the boat is crunching her way to windward. The situation eases a few days into a cruise as you acclimatise to the motion, but early on it can be grim. Do all you can to cook or prepare meals in advance. Sandwiches (not too rich or ambitious), meat pies, high-energy chocolate, biscuits, fruit, are all one-handed to eat and have only to be passed up the companionway. If your crew will fancy a real meal, pre-cook a stew that will merely require heating up and whacking into bowls or, if the going is rough, large mugs. Clamp the pan on the cooker before you leave harbour.

Such considerations also keep washing-up at sea to a minimum. A lifesaver for a beleaguered galley volunteer.

Briefing the crew

Having sorted out the passage plan and bent on suitable canvas, the last job before slipping your lines is to brief the crew. If you're skipper of a boat full of strangers, you

▶ A careful briefing is an important start when it comes to keeping the crew happy.

ought to give them a full safety brief as well as letting them into the secret of where you're bound. For a regular group of family or friends, this might be less suitable.

The formal briefing

I've listened to a great many briefings in my work as an examiner. Some are technically correct but so elongated that the troops have given up listening long before the end. Others have concentrated so hard on the 'doom and gloom' aspects of seafaring in small craft that I feared the skipper might end by adopting a 'flight attendant/emergency exit' pose and invite me to 'follow the blue lights to the place of execution'. A third group have managed to hit the right combination of brisk efficiency and a positive, caring attitude. Their briefs engender a feeling of security and team spirit, and I suspect the secret of their success is that they have asked themselves what they are trying to achieve.

The purpose of a briefing is to ensure that all hands know what to expect from the day and to give them any information essential to their safety. That's all. If the skipper starts telling them everything he knows about liferaft drills and how to behave during a helicopter casualty transfer or under heavy strafing from enemy aircraft, he's not doing the job properly. Specifics like that can be handled if they ever crop up. Here is a suitable list for a day sail with people who do not know the boat:

BRIEFING CHECKLIST

- **Destination** Distance, time scale and probable conditions. Items of interest that will be passed on the way.

- **Lifejackets** Everyone must either have a lifejacket, or know where one that fits is to be found at short notice. Non-swimmers can be issued with their personal lifer and encouraged to wear it on deck.

- **Harnesses** Ditto.

- **Special needs** Find out in as casual a way as you can whether any of your crew have special needs, particularly medical ones. You need to know who has a heart condition when you're designating muscle jobs, and it helps to be aware of which poor soul is making weekly visits to the chiropractor. Ask now if you haven't managed to elicit the information more subtly.

- **Back-up skipper** Someone must be able to take over if you go mad or become otherwise unavailable for command, even if it is only to call for help.

- **Engine start procedure** Put brutally, the crew might need power after you have fallen over the side.

- **VHF** One of the complete skipper's skills is to be able to send a distress message via VHF radio. Many boats have a card that sets out how to do this step by step. This is an excellent policy. Assuming your boat has one, you have only to indicate how to switch on the set and activate the transmitter. The instructions will do the rest. Demonstrate the lat/long readout on the GPS, because a distress broadcast will require this.

- **Flares** Demonstrate where these are stowed.

- **Liferaft** If there is one, briefly indicate how it is launched, stressing that the painter* must be tied on.

- **Fire drill** Make the point that if fire is discovered, all hands should muster on deck and that one person will remain below to fight the fire, ensuring he/she has a clear path to a safe exit lest the blaze run out of control. Show where the extinguishers are sited, and mention the galley fire blanket.

- **Galley safety** Point out the ship's policy regarding gas on/off valves.

- **Heads and seacocks** Make sure everyone knows how to use the heads and can handle any relevant seacocks. People unused to boats, and who are not confident about working this device, become embarrassed, and many would rather suffer than admit it.

- **Call to arms** Because much of the material in a boat brief is inevitably about what can go wrong, make a point of finishing on a positive note – 'Well, that's got that out of the way. Now let's go sailing!'

Informal briefings

Like many of us, I normally sail with the same people. They know what's where and what is expected of them in an emergency. A typical brief under these circumstances takes in where we are going, the weather and what sort of day we are expecting. Any more formal matter, perhaps about an item of safety gear that has been changed, I try to deal with casually in the early stages of a passage, but making absolutely sure that all who need to know do know. This way of dealing with things helps to lighten up the atmosphere which, as we have noted, can easily be rendered less than fun-filled by a heavy, prolonged brief.

● CONDUCTING THE YACHT ON PASSAGE

Navigation

Leaving harbour, you'll be in 'eyeball pilotage mode'. If the breeze is workable, the sails will be hoisted outside and you'll either set course for your first waypoint, or steer off along the coast. Have a good look round to make sure you are not at risk of collision, then hand over the helm, go below and log your departure with time, distance reading, etc. Don't enter a course if you are still steering by eye. There's no point. To keep my record straight, I write 'P' for pilotage in the course column when I'm not steering by the compass.

The priority now is to enjoy the passage and make sure your crew do as well. Relax and sail the boat. The only requirements are to know that the yacht is in safe water, travelling in the right direction, and that you can work out a position at any time. If the leg is a long one with no particular features, estimate your position every hour or so in fair weather, by guesstimate if you are confident you'll be about right. Then take and plot a GPS fix, hit the sounder for confirmation, and scrutinise any visible land or seamarks to make sure they stack up with the fix. If you have a destination waypoint, note the distance and bearing to double-check the lat/long plot, make sure the course coincides with that given on the waypoint readout, then duck back out on deck again. Your task as navigator is complete for the time being.

Sailing amongst navigational aids, each relevant one is logged as it comes by, and confirmed by a glance at the GPS and depth.

Don't forget that the most important reason for logging everything is to supply a fresh starting point – a last known position – to be used if you should lose all your main instruments. In moderate or poor visibility, it therefore makes sense to plot more frequently. To pass close by a buoy in visibility of less than a mile and fail to log it, is very slack navigational practice indeed. Even if you're busy on deck, it doesn't take more than a couple of minutes to pop below, check the log and plot the fix the buoy effectively offers you. The more often you carry out these routine procedures, the more practised you will be and the slicker you become.

While honing your navigational techniques, and even long afterwards, it pays to take visual fixes with the handbearing compass from time to time, checking their accuracy against the GPS. The reason for this is not to suggest that the GPS needs to be verified with a magnetic fix, but rather to develop your traditional skills in case they are ever needed. I grew up in a world where there was no electronic navigation of any sort. In those days, we were able practitioners of the classical fixing techniques. Now, like most people, I favour GPS for my primary fixing tool. As a result, my ability to read a coastline and relate it to a chart has been eroded. This is inevitable, but it makes the point that if you never develop the ability at all, it will be too late to start learning when you suddenly find you have nothing else. So put in some effort on the time-honoured methods. Who knows. You may even become one of those individuals who take pride in making the occasional passage without GPS at all.

Keeping an eye on the ball

The most common mistake made by prospective Day Skippers is to spend too long below decks. The arrival of GPS should have changed all that but, like the PC which was meant to do away with paper, even GPS has its own contrary tendency to create work. Nobody tells a neighbour, 'I'm just off down to the boat for a weekend's navigation.' People 'go sailing', and that's what you must keep in mind. Quite apart from the pleasure aspect, the safe skipper is one who realises this, deals with the navigation crisply and when it is needed, then carries on sailing a boat, not a chart table.

Out on deck, simple observation of natural transits can anticipate tactical decisions regarding how the yacht is being set by a current; you can also spot a potential collision when it's still miles away, attend to sail trim and ensure the helmsman does not lose it and gybe 'all standing'. You are also less likely to become debilitated by seasickness, and can see to it that vital agendas such as feeding time are given their proper priority. Don't be a chart-table skipper. Be a sailor, bronzed by the wind, developing a sharp seaman's eye for all that's going on.

Living with an electronic chart plotter

There's nothing wrong with making full use of a chart plotter. However, if this is your choice, it's vital that you maintain a paper log book so that if all fails, you have a recently logged position from which to revert to traditional methods. Nothing is then lost. From this it will be obvious that the boat must also carry a reasonable set of paper charts, not only as a backup and for planning purposes, but also to give the sort of overview that plotters aren't very good at.

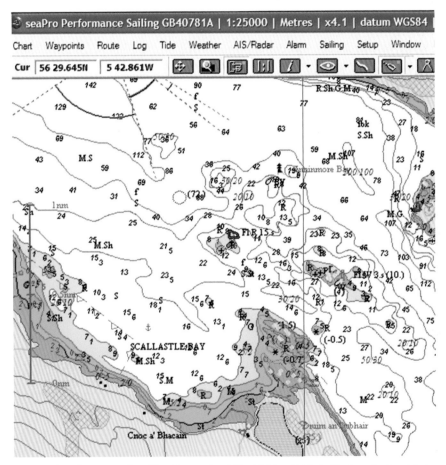

▶ A good quality vector chart like this one should be highly reliable in Western Scotland, but it still pays to have the paper chart to hand, just to make sure.

Electronic chart packages always fire up with a dire disclaimer about the fate that awaits those who rely on the product. While there is obviously a certain amount of 'making sure the producer is covered' here, there remain sound reasons for the warning. Electronic charts may not be kept up to date, and vector charts are not immune from leaving out vital data or, occasionally, being just plain wrong. This is uncommon in well-frequented waters, but numerous cases are on record of yachts coming unstuck away from the beaten track by relying on electronics without checking the paper.

LIVING ABOARD ON PASSAGE

Cold, sick and tired

Sometimes it's sunny in UK waters. More often it's anything but. Daylight passages do not often involve the need for sleep, but it's important to realise that on a chilly day people need shelter from the elements if they're going to be out there for more than three or four hours. In cold northerlies, the break point for misery may be a much shorter time than that.

Watch for crew getting cold, because this can lead to hypothermia, a clinical condition that can ultimately kill and will sap efficiency and energy even in its milder manifestations. The problem is usually that a person is too afraid of seasickness to go below, take a rest and warm up. There is a sort of short-term common sense in this. Most of us feel some tendency to motion sickness in rough seas, and there's no doubt that it's worse if we leave the fresh air behind. Unfortunately, hypothermia does more harm than seasickness although the body may be claiming otherwise, so the crew must be encouraged to go below from time to time. The best answer if you're feeling 'Tom and Dick' is to not to allow your condition to deteriorate by trying to undress, but to pile straight into a lee bunk, grab a sleeping bag and drag it on top of you. As soon as your head is down, you are actually as immune from the dreaded malaise as if you were on deck. Encourage the team to do this every so often, and take a half-hour yourself when your presence isn't demanded on deck. Leave the mate in charge and curl up with a good book even if you aren't tired enough to nod off.

Seasickness remedies

There are many of these. Certain folks react positively to one, others will find it ineffective. I would suggest trying a number of different products, but that which-ever you choose, read the instructions, check for side effects and do what it says on the packet. If you are advised to start the tablets the day before, don't wait until you are about to throw up, pop a pill, then say the stuff's no good.

My second observation is that when I worked at the National Sailing Centre (since closed down by a government with other priorities), I ran a two-year experiment. Over the first season, I offered no advice about seasickness. The second summer, I encouraged my cruising students to take Stugeron tablets exactly as per the box. These administer a small dose of a drug developed for inner ear problems, which happens also to be the root of motion sickness. They are not anti-histamines which often cause drowsiness. The effect was a startling reduction in misery. I took the things myself and felt better too. It didn't work for everyone, of course, and one otherwise reasonable chap was convinced my pills actually caused him to be ill. I use the drug to this day aboard light, modern boats, however, because in bad seas these still make me feel queasy in a way unheard of aboard the heavy traditional craft that are my private delight.

Minimising the breakages below

When the boat is heeled over, always place items you are using in the galley (mugs awaiting hot water, pans being filled, etc.) firmly against a 'downhill' fiddle*. If they are left mid-surface, they will slide, fetch up short against the fiddle and spill. The non-slip matting on sale at many chandlers is a great help.

The same rule holds good on deck. Chock your tea against the cockpit coaming*, or stand the mug against a handy sheet coil that nobody is interested in. Don't leave it where it can slide.

My own crew complain that I always order a tack immediately after the latest round of drinks has been served up. The result is at least one mug spilled for certain. Try to do better. Wait until the genoa is sheeted home. Promote peace and goodwill.

SKIPPER'S TIP	SAFETY FIRST IN THE GALLEY

In anything other than calm conditions, the cook is well advised to wear oilskin bottoms while working at a hot stove. This policy has prevented many a nasty scalding when an unexpected wash knocks a pan over.

Keeping the children busy

Many of us sail with children. Not all kids take to yachting, and if you have sired a congenitally non-sea person, I can offer little consolation other than to hire a weekend child minder or sell the yacht and take up skydiving. Most children below teenage enjoy boating, however. There are many ways of assisting them, but if your attitude is right, all else will follow.

The answer seems to be that if you think about them as small crew members, they will react well. Find them things to do that involve them with the main event. We already have them on ensign duty and in charge of fenders. Encourage them to work sails as thinking trimmers, not just extensions of your own arms. Get them on the helm as soon as you can. Boys love this. They aren't old enough to drive on the roads yet, but they can actually be in charge of a big yacht. Wow!

Send them off in the dinghy in harbour, on a string if need be, but get them away 'in charge' under oars. Do not under any circumstances let them play in an outboard-powered craft. A lad buzzing round a marina or anchorage not only

▶ A glance through the porthole reveals that the author's yacht is securely alongside. If he were at sea, he wouldn't be taking so cavalier an approach to boiling water!

infuriates those in search of a tranquil afternoon by creating mindless noise and wash, he also learns little or nothing, and rapidly becomes bored. Under oars, he discovers his limitations, he finds out about current, and takes on board the sweet humility that comes with understanding that nature is stronger than he is. He also hears the birds calling, although he may not notice it at the time. Ultimately, he becomes a better sailor, one less likely to crunch his boat and better company round the saloon table.

● EVALUATING

We've already dealt with the physical aspects of arriving in port in Chapter 8, but we saved one important matter for the real passage. After you are securely moored, take a few quiet minutes to evaluate your experience. Be frank with yourself, because this is where you learn your lessons.

How did it go? Give yourself a pat on the back for things that went well, and honestly debrief the things that are nagging you. You probably know why they weren't so good, so consider deeply how something came about and how a manoeuvre or decision could have been improved. Don't fall into the gaping trap of self-justification. It is so easy to say, 'Well, of course, if the tide hadn't been eddying by the dock, I would not have smashed into that yacht as I came alongside. It was just bad luck.'

▶ Give the kids a job, even when coming ashore, but never let them go and play with an outboard because they won't learn much. Give them a pair of oars instead.

Not a bit of it. The truth is, you didn't read the water. If you'd looked closely, there might have been some sign of the eddy. Even if there wasn't, you ought to have realised all wasn't well as you approached the berth and the contrary stream suddenly picked you up. At that point, you should have aborted and stood off to think it out. There's no harm in that, and every sailor alive has made similar mistakes. The trick is only to make them once.

So don't fool yourself. Not for a second. What happens in a yacht you are skippering is almost invariably down to you. That's one of the charms of seafaring. There's no escape from yourself. On the other hand, you get all the credit when things go well, and go well they surely will – more and more often, but only if you are ready to learn from your mistakes in those private moments of soul-searching after the crew have all turned in.

▶ All skippers, however experienced, should take the time to evaluate each significant passage or manoeuvre. Consider whether it could have been improved, and make sure all inherent lessons have been learned.

12

ADVANCED NAVIGATION

In this chapter we will gather up a number of navigational techniques thus far set aside in the cause of readily achievable progress. It is perfectly possible to make modest cruises without all this material. The secret of learning as you go, however, is to maintain a lively interest in your own limitations. While you might rub along for a while without mastering some of the issues below, they remain important building blocks towards complete confidence as you venture further afield.

● FURTHER TIDAL HEIGHT THEORY

Secondary ports

In Chapter 3 we described how tidal height predictions are tabulated for a few standard ports, each of which has satellite secondary ports whose data are determined by reference to them. We let matters stand at that for the time being, and picked up a set of local tables from the chandler. Once you set out from home, however, you cannot stow copies of the tables for every creek or harbour you might perhaps visit. An ability to deduce secondary port data from the almanac is therefore of genuine value.

The heavenly committee which planned our planet couldn't arrange for universally regular tidal differences. Often, these vary with springs and neaps, but the variations are at least consistent (Fig 12.1). The illustration shows the entry from the *Reeds Nautical Almanac* for the Beaulieu River on the West Solent. Don't worry about all the various notes near the top. The first bit you're interested in is the standard port which, in this case, is Portsmouth. The arrow shows you which way to turn the pages to get to it. The High and Low Water figures given under the heading 'Times' are the hours of Mean* High and Low Water springs and neaps (MHWS and MLWN, etc). The heights to the right of them are the mean heights for Portsmouth itself, not the secondary port.

Times

Inspect the figures below 'Stansore Point'. Beneath 0000 and 1200 (at the top) you'll see –0050. This means that if High Water at Portsmouth comes at midnight or noon, you must subtract 50 minutes from it to find the time for Stansore Point. Thus, HW

9.2.20 BEAULIEU RIVER

Hampshire **50°46'·89N 01°21'·72W** (Ent) ❀❀☙☙☙✿✿✿

CHARTS AC *5600, 2036, 2035, 2021*; Imray C3, C15; Stanfords 11, 24, 25; OS 196

TIDES –0100 and +0140 Dover; ML 2·4; Zone 0 (UT)

Standard Port PORTSMOUTH (⟶)

Times				Height (metres)			
High Water		Low Water		MHWS	MHWN	MLWN	MLWS
0000	0600	0500	1100	4·7	3·8	1·9	0·8
1200	1800	1700	2300				
BUCKLER'S HARD							
–0040	–0010	+0010	–0010	–1·0	–0·8	–0·2	–0·3
STANSORE POINT							
–0050	–0010	–0005	–0010	–0·8	–0·5	–0·3	–0·1

NOTE: Double HWs occur at or near springs; the 2nd HW is approx 1¾ hrs after the 1st. On other occasions there is a stand which lasts about two hrs. The predictions refer to the first HW when there are two, or to the middle of the stand. See 9.2.11.

▶ Fig 12.1 Secondary port. Extract reproduced from the Reeds Nautical Almanac.

Stansore Point for noon will be 1200 minus 0050 = 1110. Unfortunately, things are rarely this convenient, and you'll see that the figure beneath 0600 and 1800 is a different one. In practice the time probably won't be one of those in the book, which leaves you with a figure somewhere between the differences tabulated. The process of working out these sort of numbers is called 'interpolation'. Instructors have evolved a number of methods for handling this. I do it in my head, as follows:

For the High Water difference, I note the split in time between the two difference values (under 'Stansore Point') for standard port High Water and divide this figure by the number of hours between them. The answer, invariably counted in minutes, is how much the difference advances or retreats per hour. Next, I assess how many hours I have moved on from the earlier of the two figures, multiply that by the hourly rate of change and apply the answer to the earlier figure in the book. Explaining mathematics has never been my strong point, so let me give you an example:

Find the time of HW Stansore Point. HW Portsmouth is at 1600

Differences given for Stansore Point are –0050 (at 1200) and –0010 (at 1800). The difference therefore varies by 40 minutes in 6 hours. 40 ÷ 6 = 7 (more or less). Therefore the difference changes by around 7 minutes with each hour of HW time.

With HW at 1200 the difference is –50 minutes; if HW is at 1800 it is only –10 minutes. With HW at 1600 it will vary from the 1200 figure by 4 hours-worth, or 4 x 7 minutes = 28 minutes. This is to be subtracted from the minus 50-minute figure because we are moving towards minus 10 minutes. By nothing more than common sense, therefore, the difference with HW at 1600 can only be about minus 22 minutes.

The same basic logic works for interpolating Low Water times and for tidal height differences as well. You'll find that the more you work these calculations, the easier they become.

Given an ability to interpolate, a simple table is the best way to work secondary ports:

Referring to the information in the almanac page, find the time and height for morning LW and HW at Bucklers Hard. The Portsmouth figures for the day in question have already been lifted from the page carrying the Portsmouth tide tables. They appear on the top line of the table and you may take them as read. The tide is almost a mean Spring.

HW	TIME	HEIGHT	LW	TIME	HEIGHT
Portsmouth	1301	4.5	Portsmouth	0611	0.7
Difference Bucklers Hard	– 0035	–1.0	Difference Bucklers Hard	+ 0007	– 0.3
HW Bucklers Hard	1226	3.5	LW Bucklers Hard	0618	0.4

You'll have noticed that throughout this exercise I have been, to some extent, rounding up or down. I make no apology for this. By doing so you are unlikely to be further adrift than, perhaps, 5 minutes out of a 6-hour period, or more than 0.1 metres in height. Remember that all tidal heights and times are predictions and that local weather anomalies can and do affect them. A tide can be literally pressed down a foot or two both at High and Low Waters when atmospheric pressure is very high. Conversely, levels may be higher when pressure is low, especially in times of strong onshore wind. All tidal height calculations must therefore be applied with a sensible margin for error. Interpolating quickly in your head rather than working to fractions on paper may add a small increment to the unknown, but in reality little is lost but stress, while precious time is gained.

One final point to remember is that tidal difference data for home waters relate to GMT, not BST. If you are looking for the best possible accuracy, therefore, work your sums out in GMT, then add the BST hour to the final result.

● INTERMEDIATE TIDAL HEIGHTS

In Chapter 6 we handled the question of tidal heights between High and Low Water with the useful Rule of Twelfths. Sadly, in many areas the tide does not perform with sufficient regularity for this to be a sure-fire system. Unless you have access to a tide computer, the tidal height curves issued by the Admiralty and published in almanacs are the best answer. They are not nearly so fearsome as they appear (Fig 12.2).

Tidal curves

The illustration shows the tidal curve for Dartmouth. Note that 'time' runs along the bottom and 'height' rises up the middle. You'll see at a glance that, for this port, the 'tide rising' (left-hand) side of the graph lasts about 6½ hours whereas the ebb does its work in 5½. This irregularity alone is enough to upset the old rule of thumb. In Solent ports, the rise and fall is so eccentric that the time of High Water can be difficult to predict at all and Low Water is used as the starting point in the centre of the graph.

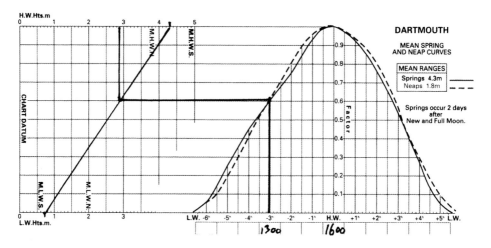

▶ Fig 12.2 Tidal height graph. Extract reproduced from the Reeds Nautical Almanac.

Here's how it works, following the example in the illustration. HW is 1600 (4.3m). LW was 0930 (0.7m):

- Write the time of HW in the box at the bottom.
- Mark the LW height on the lower height scale, and the HW height on the upper one.
- Join these two marks with a straight, diagonal line.

  The graph is now ready for use. To find the height of tide at, say 1300, continue as follows:

- Rule a vertical line from 1300 (HW −3) until it meets the curve.
- Continue across the graph until you meet the diagonal 'line of the tide'.
- Plot vertically again to the top line.
- Read off the height of tide. It is **2.9m.**

The curve can be used with equal facility to discover when a certain height will be found by starting at the height desired (upper left of diagram), working downwards to the tide line, plotting sideways from it to the curve, then dropping vertically into the time boxes.

Note that because the Low Water height is the starting point for any readings, you are reading the *height of tide*, not the *rise* above Low Water. When using the Rule of Twelfths it was necessary always to add Low Water to the rise calculated. The tidal height curve takes care of the whole issue at a stroke.

Spring and neap curves

Look carefully at the Dartmouth tidal curve and you will note a pecked-line curve running beside the main, solid line. This is the neap curve. The solid line is for springs. Use them accordingly, and if you're in between, make a visual compromise.

Tide computers

Tide computers are sold either as neat, stand-alone units or come as PC software. Both can be used for planning purposes at home and for routine tidal work on board. They are generally loaded with all the almanac information for many years to come. They will deliver intermediate heights for standard and secondary ports at the touch of a button and many can even tell you what clearance to expect above the bottom if you enter 'draught' and 'charted depth'. Not surprisingly, such powerful tools are steadily taking over from traditional methods. I see nothing but good in this, provided, as always, that you can handle the sums if the volts fail. With apologies to the poet, Sir Alan Herbert, never forget that 'the day may come, when Man's fine chattering machines are dumb.'

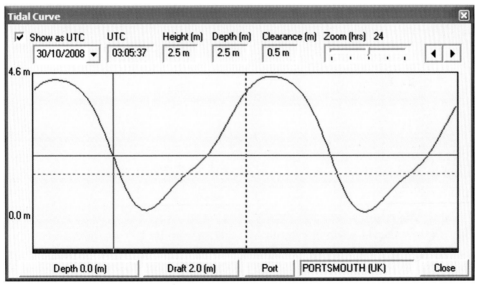

▶ A tidal curve on a PC chart plotting program. Bulkhead plotters and some hand-held variants can also generate charts like these for any day of any year.

Reduction to soundings, and other calculations

Numerous circumstances will come your way when your sounder is giving a depth that you must 'reduce to soundings'. This means working out how much tide is standing at the present time above chart datum so that you can deduce the actual charted depth at your position. A typical example is in fog, when using the sounder as a source of position line (Chapter 13). The chart is reading LAT (Chapter 3) while the echo can only give the present depth.

Reduction to soundings

To find the charted depth from an echo-sounding, you have only to glance at the tidal curve duly filled in with today's diagonal tide line, start the procedure with the real time, then run the verticals and horizontals until you reach the present tidal height. Subtract this figure from the sounded depth, making any adjustments required for transducer depth, and that is the charted sounding (Fig 12.3).

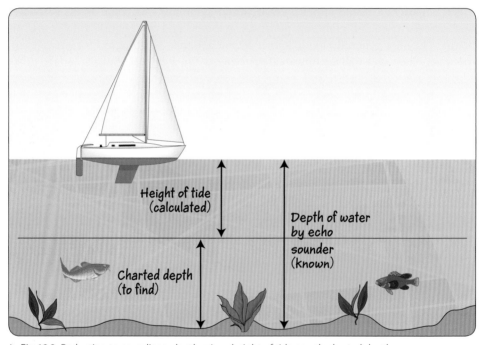

▶ Fig 12.3 Reduction to soundings: depth minus height of tide equals charted depth.

Coming to anchor

The tide calculation when coming in to anchor is similar to that for reductions to soundings, except that instead of finding how far the tide stands currently above chart datum, you want to know its height above the next Low Water (ie, its rise). Find the present height as before, then subtract the appropriate Low Water height from it. The difference is the rise of tide, which is the amount it will fall between now and Low Water. Add this to the depth you'd like to lie in at the bottom of the tide and, 'Bingo!'.

If this is racking your brain, the diagram will clarify the situation. I often draw a little picture just to remind myself exactly what it is I am trying to work out, but if you don't understand the definitions given in Chapter 6, you're a dead duck.

When the tide is rising but you intend to remain anchored over the following Low Water, a little horse sense is required. Peep over the top of the curve to look ahead to the Low Water you're interested in (Fig 12.4).

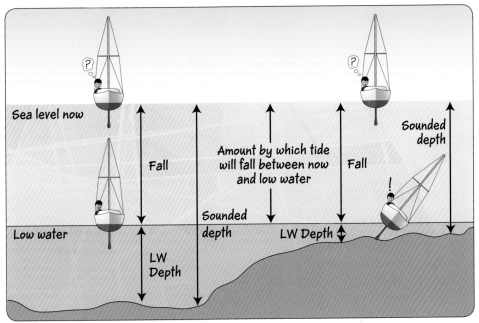

▶ Fig 12.4 Soundings for anchoring. Sounded depth on arrival is known; anticipated fall to LW is known from the tidal curve. Current depth minus the fall equals the depth at LW.

● CROSS-TIDE NAVIGATION

The tidal diamond

By far the most popular tidal stream information for coastwise small craft is the atlas pages reproduced in the almanac. However, a further source of data is to be found on many charts, where the specific survey results from which the atlases are compiled are shown. The site of the survey vessel is denoted by a capital letter in a diamond, while the data it has recorded are set out in one corner of the chart. This is referred to High Water at a standard port in 360° notation and knots, with spring and neap rates.

Being given the direction of a stream in degrees theoretically makes accurate plotting easier, but it's important to realise that the next diamond may be several miles away and will almost certainly suggest different figures. If you're somewhere

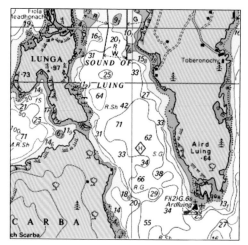

Tidal Streams referred to HW at OBAN

Hours	Geographical Position			Diamond A — 55°59'6 N, 6 30·7W		
	Directions of streams (degrees)	Rates at spring tides (knots)	Rates at neap tides (knots)			
Before High Water 6				-6	271	0·5 0·2
5				-5	354	0·5 0·2
4				-4	026	0·9 0·3
3				-3	044	1·1 0·4
2				-2	045	1·0 0·4
1				-1	059	0·7 0·2
High Water				0	081	0·3 0·1
After High Water 1				+1	183	0·3 0·1
2				+2	209	0·7 0·3
3				+3	206	1·1 0·4
4				+4	215	1·2 0·4
5				+5	236	0·8 0·3
6				+6	261	0·6 0·2

B — 56°09'2 N, 6 24·7W			C — 56°19'0 N, 6·23·2W			D — 56°12'5 N, 6 11·2W		
229	0·5	0·2	020	0·9	0·4	219	0·4	0·1
269	0·6	0·2	024	0·7	0·3	253	0·3	
293	0·8	0·3	057	0·2	0·1	282	0·1	0·1
216	0·9	0·4	153	0·2	0·1	000	0·1	0·0

▶ **Fig 12.5** Tidal diamonds give accurate data about streams on Admiralty charts. In this case, 'H' is off the picture lower down.

in between, as you usually are, the information must be interpolated, by eye, honest guess and the intuition that comes with experience.

Interpolation is also required to work out rates between springs and neaps as, indeed, it must for the atlases as well. You might choose to do this by mental arithmetic or, if you have a copy of any *Admiralty Tidal Stream Atlas* in its own booklet (as opposed to the reprint in the almanac), the option exists to use the interpolation table at the front. This works as well for information drawn from a diamond as it does for rates given in the atlas itself.

From this, you will see that the atlas is often the most practical source of usable information, and its pictorial nature also confers the advantage that the overall position can be instantly read by eye. Nevertheless, the diamonds have their place. If you are close to one, its recordings are the most accurate information you can have.

Plotting a course to steer

We learned in Chapter 2 how working a transit keeps you in a straight line when approaching a berth in a cross-current, and in Chapter 3 the same principle was applied to decide whether you are on a collision heading with another vessel. On passage, the transit remains the best way of keeping a boat on a direct track. If you can see your destination or the next mark of your route with land or some other object beyond it, the problem of cross current is immediately solved. Line it up straight away with something fixed behind it, then steer to keep it there. Even if you aren't pointing at it, so long as you, the destination and your datum point remain in line, you are tracking dead straight.

If there is no background, or you can't see where you're going, make a plot to achieve the same result. Here is the method for working up a simple course-to-steer illustrated by Fig 12.6:

1 Using a 2B pencil (clear to see, easy to erase), draw a straight line between your present position and where you want to go (a). Give it two arrowheads as the conventional sign for 'track' – your course to be made good over the bottom.

2 From the atlas or a diamond, decide what the tide will do to you in the coming hour. Depending on when you start in relation to High Water, this might be a convenient 'tidal hour' or it could be the aggregate of two half-hours from either side. Plot the tide, starting from your departure point (b). The line will be either the compass heading (true) given in the tidal diamond, or an eyeball copy of the tidal stream atlas arrow (some people lay the chart protractor on the atlas arrow before transferring it to the chart). Give the plot the same length in miles and decimals that the tide is making in knots. This 'tide vector' represents what would happen to the boat in one hour if she were left to drift.

3 Now measure off the latitude scale how far you expect to travel in the coming hour. If the traverse will be of less than an hour's duration, don't worry. Just open the dividers to your boat speed, (a knot equals a nautical mile per hour).

4 Place one divider point at the end of the tide vector and swivel the other point round until it rests on the track, which can be extended beyond the destination

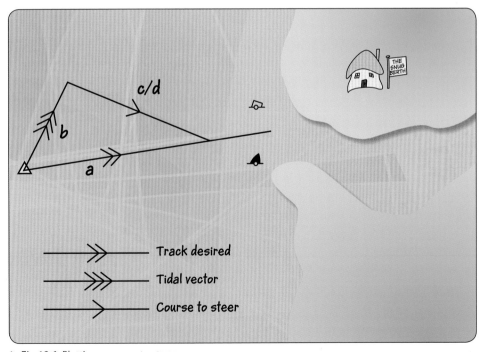

▶ Fig 12.6 Plotting a course to steer.

if need be. Scratch a mark and join this with the end of the tide line (c/d). Denote it with one arrow and measure its compass bearing. That is the course to steer to counteract the tide.

Two points of interest

■ As shown in Fig 12.6, the boat never leaves the track line if all goes well. The other lines in this vector diagram are merely constructions. So, if the course-to-steer line itself appears to cross some danger sited a safe distance from the track, do not be dismayed.

■ On no account join up the end of the tide line with your destination. If you do, your course-to-steer line will not represent an hour's run and will no longer be in harmony with the one-hour tide vector. Maintain the correct proportions by using boat speed for the course-to-steer line.

SKIPPER'S TIP   AWKWARD PLOTS

Often, you won't want an exact hour for a course to steer. You may need more, or less. If it's lots more, plot the 'tide hours' one by one, each starting at the end of its predecessor, and make sure you correspond with the right number of hours for the course-to-steer line (plotted from the end of the last tide vector). Where the leg of your passage is going to be less than an hour, or the scale of the chart renders a one-hour diagram impractical, choose any scale you like. Since the whole exercise is merely a representation of what is actually happening, you can measure 'knots' and 'miles' on the longitude scale or on some arbitrary scale inscribed on your chart protractor. It's fine to choose centimetres, inches, or the width of your thumbnail, so long as you stick with the same units throughout the diagram. If the proportions remain the same, the angles won't vary.

Estimating the position

Estimating the position in a cross-tide is really like plotting a course to steer backwards. From compass and log, you know what course has been steered and how far the boat has come along it. All that remains is to adjust it for tidal stream (Fig 12.7).

1 Ask the helm what course has been steered on average. Plot it with the distance run for an hour (one arrow), starting from your last known position (a). This is the Dead Reckoning position (DR) from Chapter 7.

2 Now determine the tidal vector for the relevant period, just as you would for course to steer.

3 Plot the tide at the 'now' end of the course steered (b). The Estimated Position (EP) is at the end of the tide line. Mark it with a triangle (c) and a time, then log it.

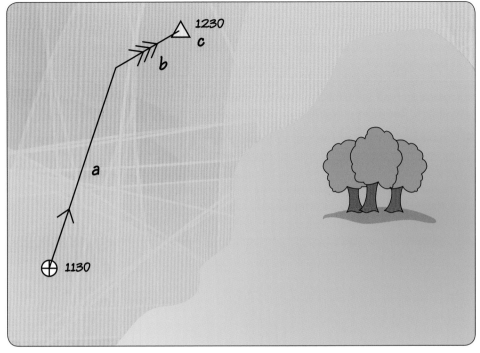

▶ Fig 12.7 Estimating position.

Special cases

■ An EP is unlike a course to steer in that you must plot 'real-time' distances. A mile is a mile on an EP. If an EP extends over more than one hour, it saves trouble to plot both DRs first, one behind the other, then plot the tidal hours, also 'in tandem', onto the composite DR.

■ Where an EP is required for less than an hour, plot the DR as required, then divide the tide vector accordingly. For example, 40 minutes in a 3-knot tide would drift you 2 miles (3 x 40/60 = 2).

Leeway

A yacht under sail is usually blown sideways to some extent by the breeze. This is called 'making leeway'. When running, she makes no leeway at all, but when reaching with the wind from the beam or forward of it, she makes more and more until the sliding reaches a maximum at closehauled. It is not easy to measure a boat's leeway, but it can be estimated by observing the wake and comparing it with some fore-and-aft line on the boat such as a hatch side or cockpit duckboard*. Typically, it reaches 7° closehauled in a deep-fin cruiser, with 10° or more being normal for a closehauled bilge-keeler. In heavy seas, the value can rise dramatically, so never underestimate it.

Compensating for leeway

- **EP** Lightly sketch the wind direction on the chart before you plot your course steered. As you place the chart protractor down to draw the course steered, rotate it away from the wind by the leeway figure, just as the boat herself is blown downwind. Now plot the line. Rather than strictly a DR, this then becomes the 'course steered adjusted for leeway'. Plot your tidal vector on the end of it and you have the most comprehensive estimate you're likely to get.

- **Course to steer** When you expect to make leeway steering a plotted course, sketch the wind on the chart as before, plot your vector diagram, then rotate the chart protractor towards the wind by the appropriate amount. This is the course you give to the helm and which you write in the log book. By steering thus to weather of the desired course, the wind should blow the yacht back onto it (Fig 12.8).

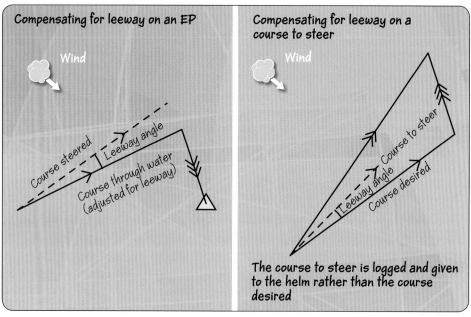

Compensating for leeway on an EP

Wind

Course steered

Leeway angle

Course through water (adjusted for leeway)

Compensating for leeway on a course to steer

Wind

Course to steer

Leeway angle

Course desired

The course to steer is logged and given to the helm rather than the course desired

▶ Fig 12.8 Leeway.

Cross-track error

Most GPS receivers feature a 'cross-track error' function which indicates how far the boat has drifted from the direct track between the point at which the function was activated and the next waypoint. It can supply a check on how the plotted cross-tide course is working out, allowing it to be modified as required. It can also provide a useful report on drift when you have not worked out the full course for some reason. The display shows which way to steer to come back onto track, but beware of this. Sometimes the advice is sound, but it may also recommend a huge course alteration to bring you back to a track you don't really need. Often, when you see you have been

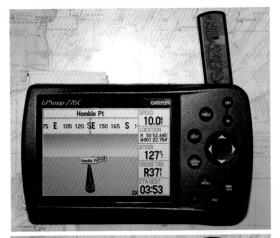

▶ Two different ways of quantifying how you are drifting from your desired track. The 'rolling road' gives the exact distance you are set to one side, a bearing to the waypoint and the current track, as well as a less useful Estimated Time of Arrival.

The alternative display may well come up when you ask the unit to 'go to' the waypoint. It is often the more practical, merely showing track, bearing and distance. If the difference between the first two items is monitored, you have a good indication of rate of drift, which can be less distracting than the exacting demands of the rolling road.

set off the track, it is better to plot the new position, make sure that the track from this to the waypoint in question is free of obstruction, then re-activate the cross-track error. It should reset and start from scratch again, saving you a needless detour.

Cross-track error can be an effective tool, but it has a tendency to become obsessive. It may be a life-saver running down the final few hundred yards to a mark in fog, but in wider circumstances, the same result can be more usefully obtained by comparing an altered bearing to the waypoint with one noted a few minutes ago. Cross-track error is, after all, only an electronic means of delivering the same information as your eyes do when steering down a transit. For sheer 'usability' a natural visual transit beats it hollow.

● COMPASS DEVIATION

So far, we have been working on the assumption that the magnetic compass reads correctly. Unfortunately, this is not always true. The magnetised needle is held on its north-south axis by the Earth's own magnetic field, but like all magnetic devices, the compass reacts to heavy lumps of iron. These can come into the compass's sphere of influence in two ways. Their effect is known as compass 'deviation'.

The first possibility is that something like a ferrous metal screwdriver or spanner (stainless steel is magnetically inert) is left carelessly in the vicinity. All manner of unexpected items can deviate a compass. Even spectacle frames have been known to affect the handbearing variety. The answer to this is obvious, and if you have any doubt how dramatic such effects can be, try laying the ship's largest mole grips an inch or so from a compass.

The second source of compass deviation is hefty, immovable objects in the boat herself, such as engines and iron keels. Because the compass needle stays still as the boat turns beneath it, its relationship to deviating items changes with heading. They might pull the compass one way when she is on a certain heading, but another altogether as she turns. This type of deviation to the steering compass is predictable. It can be measured and, once known, applied where necessary to bring compass courses into line.

Before we go into how this is achieved, I am delighted to advise that if you sail a fibreglass production yacht, deviation is unlikely to be an issue on short passages. If it exists at all, it probably won't amount to more than two or three degrees at worst, and since much of your navigation will be visual pilotage, such finesse is rarely critical. Some yachts, particularly those built of steel or wood, can carry substantial deviation, however, so it is prudent to understand how to recognise and handle it.

Running a deviation check

It is easy to check and note deviation. Set aside an hour or so on a fine day to find a quiet patch of calm water with a distant object in clear view three or four miles away. All you need now is paper, a pencil and a handbearing compass. Handbearing compasses are subject to deviation, but because you can move them around, it's often possible to find a place on board where they are free of it. To achieve this, stand in what looks a likely site on deck and have someone steer the boat round in a circle 50 yards or so across. While they are doing this, take a steady bearing on the distant object, rotating on the spot as you do. If the bearing does not alter materially throughout the 360° turn, the handbearing compass has no deviation at the point where you are standing. You are now finished with the distant object.

Knowing the handbearing compass is reading accurately, you have only to compare it with the steering compass, and any difference must be deviation of the latter. Stay in your place and have the helmsman steer 000, 045, 090, 135, 180, 225, 270 and 315. Look straight ahead over the handbearing compass to where the boat is heading, noting its reading on each leg of the compass 'swing'. Then repeat the operation to check.

Making up a deviation card

If there is enough difference on some headings to care about, the next job is make up a deviation card.

Compare the two figures for each heading, then apply the maxim, 'error west, compass best, error east compass least', as we did for variation. 'Compass' in this context refers to the steering compass, since that is the one with the error. Deviation is taken as being an error on the magnetic bearing, so 'magnetic' is the starting point. No need to muddy the waters by bringing in 'true' here. Thus if the steering compass reads 045°M while the handbearing was 049°, the deviation is 4° east ('compass least, error east'). Had the handbearing read a lower value, the deviation would have been west.

The results of this check are plotted on a simple graph as shown (Fig 12.9).

Many yachts have had deviation checks performed by professional compass adjusters. Their deviation cards are usually numerical in form, listing a series of headings and the relevant deviations.

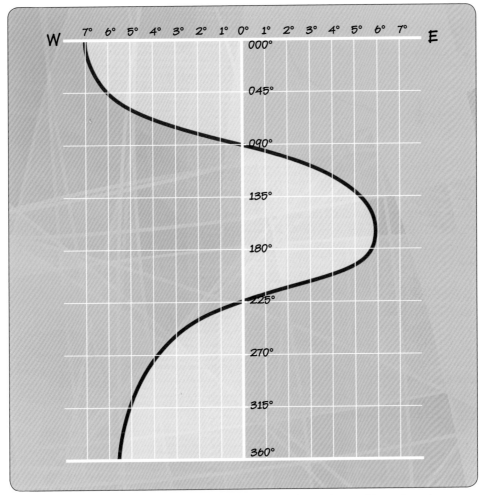

▶ Fig 12.9 A deviation card. This is from a steel boat; most modern yachts would experience less deviation.

Compensating for deviation

In Chapter 6, we established that a heading is expressed as 'True' when it relates directly to the Earth's geographical grid, or 'Magnetic' if it has been corrected for compass variation. Where it is relevant, the final stage in this process is to correct the magnetic course for deviation, thus converting it to what is called a 'Compass' heading, expressed as, for example, '090°C'. There is no mystery about this procedure. The favourite stumbling block is to forget that deviation is applied to magnetic values, and that variation is applied only to true. You cannot get from 'true' to 'compass' without working through the intermediary of 'magnetic', or vice versa. As we have seen, the same basic rules for adjusting the heading apply. Here are a couple of examples:

> Course from the chart is 065T
> Variation 4°W
> Deviation 7°W
> 065T + 4 (variation west, compass best)
>   = 069M + 7 (deviation west, compass best) = 076C

> Course steered has been 280C
> Deviation 6°E
> Variation 4°W
> 280C + 6 (deviation east, compass least)
>   = 286M – 4 (variation west, compass best)
>   = 282T

To correct all the way from compass to true or vice versa, you might prefer to side-step the double whammy by making a sum of the two errors and applying it singly to one or the other:

Variation 6°W
Deviation 9°E
Net compass error = 3°E
A true heading of 180T thus becomes 177C,
Or a compass course of 245C becomes 248T

● ELECTRONIC CHART PLOTTERS

An electronic chart plotter is a different animal from the protractor – traditionally called a 'plotter' – which we all use for defining courses and fixes on 'paper' charts. It is an instrument linking an electronic chart on a computer screen with various inputs, including GPS. By indicating the yacht's 'real-time' position continually and with great accuracy, it does away with the need to plot fixes. Waypoints can be inserted at the click of a mouse and routes can be created and monitored.

Perhaps the greatest marvel is the 'projected track' feature. This is often left un-activated because it can only be found at the bottom of a pile of menus deep in the machine's systems. Make sure you avoid such a tragedy by making a point of discovering the right button. Once set up, the boat on the screen will have a line projecting from her bow indicating exactly where she is currently tracking. This is what navigators have been desperate to know since Noah's day. Now it's available (for very little money in real terms) so if you've got it, do use it.

In these and other ways, the chart plotter can superficially appear to render traditional navigation skills redundant, but in reality it does nothing of the sort. The truth is that only a simpleton would capitulate to the plotter's powers. For all its excellence and desirability, a plotter cannot yet make strategic decisions or think for you beyond the essential mathematics. Indeed, you must ask yourself if you would really want it to. If you choose to install one as your main system, it is therefore essential to develop basic proficiency first. Without this, you will not understand what sort of questions you should be asking it, or how to instigate remedial action should it fail.

Because plotters can refer back to previous positions it is tempting for those using them to abandon the discipline of the log book. As we've already noted, don't! Apart from the social loss of not knowing when the skipper changed his socks last or why the mate was denied a second helping of spotted dick, you will be left totally in the dark should the plotter go down. At least enter a lat/long position every hour, log your distance run, note all headings, and on no account go to sea without a full folio of paper charts as back-up.

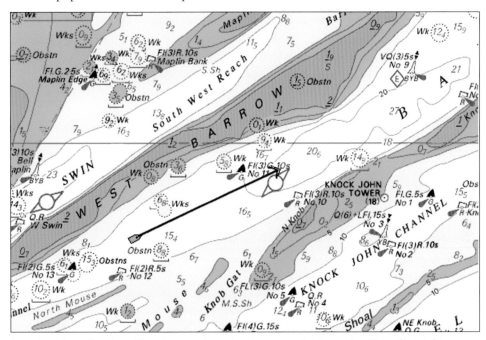

▶ A plotter's predicted track function can show at a glance exactly where a boat is tracking right now.

● CORRECTING CHARTS

The rocks may not move, but buoys marking them do; light characteristics are changed; sand banks and shipping lanes shift. Such alterations are collated by cartographers and corrections issued four times annually in the form of Small Craft Notices to Mariners. If you are conscientious enough to use these, make any corrections specified, then note the number and date of each one in the bottom left-hand corner of the chart. These details can give you a good idea of whether a chart you are using is in fact up to date.

If you haven't downloaded the Notices, at least check major buoys and beacons against those given in the almanac. This source of information might not be as good as the real thing, but it has the merit of at least being ready to hand. It was also in date at the time of publication, which won't be more than a year ago.

When you suspect your chart may be compromised in the matter of corrections, you must be circumspect in all decisions relating to navigation aids and the sort of sandy or muddy shoal that looks as though it might wander every time there is a gale. Be prudent, giving uncertain areas a wide berth and leaving plenty of depth clearance if in the slightest doubt. Better still, put your hand in your pocket and buy a new chart!

Most electronic charts are easily corrected by those with the funds to buy the software. Some of the cheaper plotter programs keep the loot rolling in for their manufacturers by going out of date and refusing duty until you have bought a fresh set of charts. In any event, it is important to check out the correction deal at the time of buying into a system. So much precision is assumed of electronic charts that it is perhaps even more important to keep them in date than their paper equivalent, whose owners have traditionally not been without sin when it comes to implementing the latest word from the cartographers.

13

FOG

Everybody hates fog. It strikes unease into even the stoutest heart, but with GPS it is far less of a challenge than ever before. Even without electronics, the application of a modest degree of education can save the day.

The first message is the most important one. If 'fog banks' are big in the weather bulletin, the forecasters generally mean what they say. Stay in harbour and take the opportunity to treat your engine to an oil change. 'Fog patches' might catch you out, but if you don't have far to go and things look reasonably clear right now, you might choose to take a calculated risk. When you are caught out by fog at sea, your duties fall into the three categories of safety, tactics and navigation.

● SAFETY IN FOG

In the days before electronic fixing, updating the plot topped the list when fog seemed to be closing in, because a recent fix to confirm the EP was essential before tactics could even be considered. With the yacht's position in the bag, the skipper could look next to the crew's personal safety before deciding such issues as whether to change the destination. Now that an accurate fix is permanently available, the navigation side of things is a great deal less fraught, so safety can take its proper place at the head of the list. Here are the various actions that must be attended to in these special circumstances:

See and be seen

Looking out

One of your duties under the international collision regulations is to maintain an extra lookout in fog. In a small boat, this really means designating at least one person, in addition to the helmsman, to do nothing but watch and listen. Danger can come from any direction, but the most likely one is from ahead, so the extra lookout will ideally be stationed forward of the mast. This may not be sensible in rough going, but try to do the best you can.

Looking out in fog means more than just peering into the mist. Listening is almost more important. Keep your ears open for fog horns and engines. It pays to

▶ A misty morning after a cold damp night. But this type of fog often burns off as the sun rises.

slow the boat every so often for a really good 'listen', because even on the foredeck away from the racket of the yacht's own motor, the bow wave can mask the noise of what's coming.

Radar is not part of the Day Skipper syllabus, but if your boat is equipped with it you are obliged to use it in fog. If need be, therefore, buy one of the excellent handbooks for yacht radar operation and go on a weekend radar course as soon as possible.

Fog signals from ships and boats

Any power-driven vessel under way gives out one long blast every two minutes. If she is a ship, this will be the characteristic roar of a siren. A small yacht will be using either a compressed-air canister device or a small trumpet like a huntsman's horn. It's easy to remember the signal by the mnemonic, 'here I come, sounding one!'.

Two long blasts means a power-driven vessel that is not making way, but not anchored or moored either, in other words, drifting with the current.

Any vessel under sail, fishing, towing, or generally hampered in some way uses the single letter Morse-code signal 'D' which means 'I am manoeuvring with difficulty'. This takes the form of one long followed by two short blasts and is also sounded every couple of minutes. Don't make the common mistake of sounding 'D' when you're under power (Fig 13.1).

One long blast every 2 minutes - power driven vessel

One long and two short blasts - sailing, fishing, towing etc.
This is the morse code for 'D' - "I am manoeuvering with difficulty".

▶ Fig 13.1 Sound signals in fog.

Anchored in fog, a vessel under 100 metres long theoretically rings a bell. Anything over this length bangs a gong from aft as well ('at anchor and long, a bell and a gong'), although such signals are rarely heard nowadays.

If a yacht is under 12 metres, she is in theory absolved from making specific signals, but is required to make some efficient sound at least every two minutes. In practice, most comply with the regulations for larger craft. It's just as easy, and everyone knows what's happening when they hear us coming.

Extra precautions

Often, fog is accompanied by calm conditions, leaving you motoring. Hoist your mainsail whether you need it or not. It will help others to see you in the murk. Turn on the navigation lights as well, making sure you use the steaming light halfway up the mast as well as the side and stern lights if you are motoring. Never use a tricolour masthead light at the same time as the sidelights or the steaming light. It is there to conserve battery power when under sail alone and is used at no other time.

Finally, always carry a radar reflector and hoist it in fog if it isn't permanently rigged aloft. A sailing yacht doesn't make much of a radar target and you may not be as visible as you'd like, to ships or fishing craft relying on this form of lookout. The reflector will multiply your chances of being spotted.

Ready for the worst

When the weather thickens, the greatest peril lies in the possibility of being run down. If this ultimate disaster should befall, there may not be time to find the crew's lifejackets, so have them wear these at all times in fog. Falling overboard is also doubly dangerous, for the obvious reason that the casualty will very soon be lost to view, so if you have any doubt, clip on as well.

● FOG TACTICS

Fog generally leaves a skipper with a choice of three tactical options. The first is to carry on to the intended

▶ A radar reflector can either be permanently rigged or, if you don't like the way it looks, the weight aloft and the windage, hoist yours on a signal halyard when the weather smells like fog.

destination; the second is to peel off for an easier entry somewhere else, but if your destination has an entrance you no longer fancy and no easier alternative presents itself, the safest bet is often to head for shallow water then anchor safely clear of heavy shipping to wait for an improvement. This alternative is especially attractive where you are unsure of your position.

When deciding about the viability of different harbours in thick visibility, take into account not only navigational considerations, but also the probable density of traffic. Remember that being run down remains the greatest danger. Harbours in rivers may well prove convenient to approach in this respect because once inside and certain of where you are, it is often safe to sneak up close to the shore in water shallow enough to ensure that any commercial shipping would run aground before it hit you.

The collision regulations specify that, in restricted visibility, all vessels should proceed at what is described as 'a safe speed'. For an 18-knot power yacht this may represent a substantial reduction. For most sailing boats, the difference will be less dramatic. Common sense and feeling will tell you what you should do. Just remember that when another vessel is coming at you head on, the converging velocity may be a boat's length per second even at slow speed.

NAVIGATION IN FOG

Waypoints and GPS

The first essential about using GPS in fog is always to operate in such a way that, should the electronics fail, you have a contingency plan for extricating yourself. This may be as simple as steering a reciprocal course back to the safety of deep water or anchoring where you are, but you absolutely must know what you will do if the numbers go blank. With that axiom firmly in mind, you can proceed to work your way in.

We noted in the chapter on general navigation that good practice demands a plotted and logged position at least every hour when on passage. This is over and above any navigational aids being passed close at hand, such as buoys, which might well merit a log entry in their own right, regardless of the time of day. The policy becomes even more crucial in restricted visibility, because if your GPS fails, you will be anxious to work from the most recent position possible.

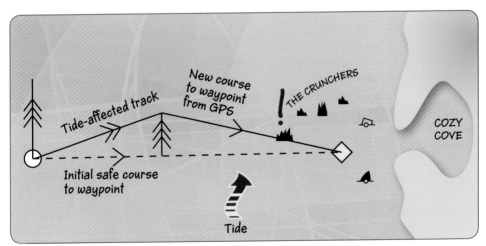

▶ Fig 13.2 A GPS-assisted shipwreck. A skipper foolish enough to follow a changing bearing blindly towards a waypoint, may be headed for disaster.

Waypoints are always useful, but they really come into their own when you can't see where you're going. Plot a waypoint somewhere beside the destination landfall, but think hard about the local significance of its exact location. Don't just automatically plant it smack in the middle of the entrance to a busy harbour. This may make sense for a quiet creek, but you don't want to arrive plumb between the buoys in Southampton Water just as the Queen Victoria steams in from New York, complete with tugs, pilot cutter and a vigilant harbourmaster in his launch.

There are two choices of technique for steering towards the destination waypoint. First, choose either the cross-track error (CTE) of the GPS or a suitable function of the electronic plotter to keep you on the initial safe track. If you're using paper charts and find CTE hard to get on with, you can alternatively work towards the waypoint by noting changes in bearing in order to check any cross-set. If you are being shunted off-track, rotate the protractor to the new bearing and lay it on the chart to make certain the direct approach to the waypoint is still safe, always keeping an eye on the depth for that double-check.

It is rare indeed for fog to shut down the visibility to less than 50 metres. In reality, it is more often 100 or even 200. This means that by the time you have arrived at the waypoint, you will often be able to see the way in. If the harbour is huge, or you are entering a big estuary, you may have to run a depth contour (see below) or buoy-hop from one navigation mark to the next. By all means use GPS to assist in finding the buoys, but don't get so bogged down plotting and entering waypoints that you lose touch with the lookout and what is going on out on deck. Remember, that is where the truth lies.

Finding a harbour without GPS

If you don't have a GPS, or the one on the bulkhead has died from salt water or lack of volts, things may not be as bad as they seem. After all, sailors have had to cope without electronics ever since Noah launched the Ark, and they didn't all come unstuck every time the fog settled on them. They employed methods that are beautiful in their logic.

After you have done what you can to fix your position, the first item on the agenda when things turn thick is the tactical decision. Is the destination free of dangers, or is it rock-bound? If the latter, don't try it unless you are very sure of yourself. Go somewhere more suitable, anchor in shallow water, or stay at sea. Where an approach is clear, you may well find it is safe to steer along a depth contour until you arrive. Entering harbour is then usually the safest option, because once you are secure alongside or moored in a recognised anchorage, the fear of being run down is virtually removed.

Running a contour to safety

This technique is a proven winner and, given the right lie of the land and sea, works every time (Fig 13.3).

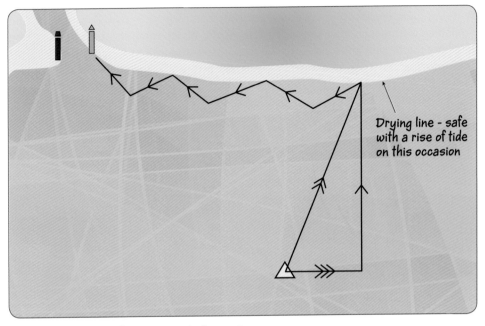

Drying line - safe
with a rise of tide
on this occasion

▶ Fig 13.3 Running a safe contour to a harbour entrance.

- Starting from a recent EP, inspect the chart to see which side of the entrance presents the more regular depth contours. One of them will probably either cross the entrance close to an identifiable mark, or change direction at the entrance to guide you safely in.

- Shape a course to miss the entrance to the desired side, making sure you come up with either the visible shore itself or a suitable depth contour.

- On the way in, carry out any calculations to reduce the current tidal height to soundings (Chapter 12). This may not be necessary if the tide is modest or you are in a position to make a rough but safe 'guesstimate' as to what tide height might be.

- When the echo sounder picks up the chosen contour, you will know which way to turn to run along it. Alter course as necessary to stay in the right depth. Had you aimed for the harbour entrance, the odds are that you would have missed it and, arriving at the desired sounding, would not know which side of it you were placed. That's why it pays to miss it on purpose.

- Sometimes, a beach or even a cliff face will be seen just within visible range as you come in from seaward. This often happens to me approaching the western end of the Solent from Christchurch Bay. Here, the shingle is so steep-to that a yacht can sail along in ten metres of water literally a biscuit's toss away from the chaps walking their dogs. Watching the beach is even easier than running a contour, but it's important to monitor the depth as well so as not to be carried away with over-confidence and end up driven onto a lee shore*.

■ If you have reason to be less than perfectly confident in your GPS system, or no viable contingency plan presents itself on the direct route in, a perfect solution where the terrain allows it, is to use the contour method to sound the way home, employing the GPS as a further check on position rather than as the primary system of navigation.

▶ Even in summer, fog banks can suddenly form. This is another good reason for keeping a lookout at all times.

14

ANCHORING, MOORING AND BOAT HANDLING

The way a boat is handled is one of the surest signs of a skipper's overall ability. Sailing along from one port to the next, one can get away with atrocities in sail trim because not only is nobody close at hand to notice, but also the boat is not required to be under especially good control while surrounded by infinite searoom. It's only in tight corners that class will out.

The most frequently required boat-handling skills are anchoring, mooring and coming alongside under power and sail. We'll deal with these first before considering one or two other procedures normally undertaken out at sea which, if managed efficiently, can make life a deal easier. The only major gyration we'll pass by is the 'man overboard pick-up'. This is the most challenging of them all, and so it is to be saved for the last 'hands-on' chapter.

● MANOEUVRES UNDER POWER

Mooring

In Chapter 2 we discussed the basics of moving into and out of a berth under power. You'll recall the principles of keeping way to a minimum and stemming the tide wherever possible. The same two axioms apply to mooring.

Before approaching a mooring, assess which way the boat will lie to it under the influences of wind and tide. This is easy if there are any other moored craft around. Pick one that has the same configuration of keel and general windage as your own, and you can bet you'll end up lying parallel with her. If no give-aways like this present themselves, observe any tide running past the buoy and approach into the stream, just as you would a marina pontoon. If the wind is blowing you along even with your sails down, be ready to go solidly astern in good time to take off way (watch out for the prop-walk!), otherwise your foredeck crew may lose their arms or the boat hook if they manage to grab the buoy. Where there's no tide, approach up-wind.

Securing to various types of mooring

■ **Pick-up buoy** Often, you'll see a small buoy, perhaps with some sort of plastic hoop on top, floating beside a mooring. Hook this and pull it aboard. As like as not, it will have a strong but weedy strop attached to it with a loop spliced into the end. Lead this 'fair' through either the bow roller or a bow fairlead, drop it over your cleat or bollard and the job's done.

▶ Always select a mooring with a pick-up buoy if one is available. It's easier to grab with the boat hook and with luck it will have a good mooring strop to drop over your cleat. Lassoing a buoy is the last resort and is, at best, only a temporary solution.

■ **Mooring ring** The second likely arrangement is a galvanised ring on top of the mooring buoy itself. These are generally to be relied on for strength. The best way of securing to a ring is often to slip a rope through quickly as you arrive, then make both ends fast on board so that you can either pull up short to the buoy, or slip at a moment's notice. It's a bad idea to lie to a slip rope overnight, however, because the arrangement is prone to chafe. Even if it doesn't chafe through, the line is often weakened slap in the middle, thus delivering you into the ever-open arms of your friendly chandler. Make fast as soon as you can using a round turn and a long bowline. The turn minimises chafe and the bowline is easy to undo once you take the load off with the engine prior to letting go. The long loop enhances accessibility and spares the backs of the foredeck hands.

One final word on buoy rings. If your team are struggling to slip that initial line through the ring, you might consider using the lasso technique described below as an alternative means of grabbing hold.

- **No attachment of any sort** If you're stuck with one of these wretches – generally large balloons with no ring or pick-up – there is little choice but to lasso the buoy. This is achieved by attaching both ends of a heavy rope to the foredeck cleats, then hanging out over one side of the bow holding the bight of the rope in both hands. The helm places the boat so the mooring comes within range on the designated side of the bow and the crew drops the bight over the buoy, waits until it sinks, then pulls one end tight. The bight will tighten around the 'riser' of the mooring and hold the yacht – on a temporary basis only. Do not lie for long like this. Not only is it potentially insecure, the rope can chafe the mooring itself, causing despair to the rightful owner and rage to the harbourmaster.

Lassoing buoys is a useful last resort for short-term mooring. It is definitely not the first thing a proper sailor thinks of. Always choose a pick-up buoy or ring if there is one.

Anchoring

Anchors are imagined by the public at large to hold a ship in position by virtue of weight alone. This is far from true. The only reason an anchor is heavy is to encourage it to claw its way into the seabed. Once well dug in, a good 'hook' takes a lot of shifting.

In order to plough into the bottom, the anchor must be pulled in with plenty of horizontal grunt. The anchor is attached to the boat by a 'cable', which may be either chain or rope. If rope, it should be nylon, selected for its huge strength and springy, shock-absorbing properties. It must also have a length of chain between the rope and the anchor, both to weigh down the hook as it bites in and to resist

▶ Beware of anchoring in deep weed. If the hook fails to take twice and comes up looking like this, consider going elsewhere.

chafe at the seabed. The chain will be of the short-link variety in galvanised steel, and the heavier it is, the better it will do its job.

Whatever boat you buy, if she is new, the builder will almost certainly have specified inadequate ground tackle. This is to save him money and to economise on weight. If you are intending to sleep at anchor enjoying any sort of peace of mind, you will probably be well advised to upgrade by at least one hop. When I first went off cruising, my 32ft boat had been realistically equipped by my experienced predecessor. She toted a 32lb CQR as her number one (bower) anchor, backed up by 45 fathoms (85 metres to you) of ⅜in (10mm) chain. She never dragged unless I asked the impossible of her. By contrast, the 32-footers I used to work at a well-known sailing school had 25lb CQRs and 40 metres of ⁵⁄₁₆ (8mm) chain. Admittedly, they were somewhat lighter in displacement, but it was a different world. They dragged all round the English Channel, and they were better equipped than many!

▶ A modern Spade anchor. These deliver great holding power and have the advantage of the heavy end being dismountable, making them easy to stow below, if that's what you want.

Scope

Both chain and rope cables should be marked to indicate how much you are using. I paint my chain every ten metres each season. One good splash at 10, two at 20, and so on. Some people label at 5-metre intervals, but I find this fussy. Ten metres is around a boat's length. You'll never lay less than that, and with 10-metre mark intervals, you can generally see one or the other and guess the rest.

When setting an anchor, you must first decide how much cable to let go. The ratio of length to depth of water is called the 'scope'. Heavy chain stretched out between a boat and her anchor hangs down into a swooping curve called a catenary by virtue of its own weight. This gives a strong horizontal component to the pull on the anchor, so less cable is required than if the cable were rope, which pulls more or less in a straight line diagonally downwards from the boat.

For chain, a ratio of 3 or 4:1 (at High Water) is a good starting point. I rarely lay more than this and, with my heavy tackle, even more rarely experience any problems. With rope, it is a different story, with 6 or 7:1 being a sensible working scope. In either case, if you expect high winds, lay more. In fact, so long as you don't mind heaving it back up again in the morning and there is no danger that an unexpected wind shift might swing you into the snuggery of the Sailor's Return, the more scope you lay, the merrier you shall be.

Setting the anchor

The selection of a site for anchoring is a considerable skill, but fortunately it is based firmly on observing the obvious. As in all seamanship, consider the worst-case scenario. Look for shelter from waves, seas or swell first, then from the wind. See to it that you do not end up anchored off a lee shore, then take a good look round and consider your probable swinging circle. You cannot rely on all your neighbours waltzing around the same way that you do, so leave plenty of space, particularly in rivers where wind and tide are likely to become opposed. Anyone who has experienced the ghastly nocturnal couplings of yachts in Dartmouth Harbour and similar river anchorages knows exactly what I mean.

Having decided where to let go, approach with your bows heading the way you anticipate they will point once you're anchored. Essentially, this means up-tide if there is any, or up-wind if there isn't. Look at other boats as you do for a mooring, make sure there's plenty of space, stop the boat when you arrive on the spot, then lower the anchor.

Your sole task now is to ensure that the ironmongery takes a firm grip into the bottom. You'll already have worked out how much cable you want. Rope can be paid out evenly, chain is a bigger challenge. If the yacht has a windlass, let the chain go under control as you manoeuvre away slowly astern. The tendency to dump it all in a heap is to be avoided, because you may end up lying to a pile of chain, never digging in the anchor until it is too late. Where you have no windlass, range the desired length out on the side deck, make the bight fast at the chosen point and let it run when the time comes, always bearing in mind the danger of a pile-up. It cannot be over-stressed that a running chain is highly dangerous. Treat it with the gravest respect and warn the crew to do likewise. Many a full-time sailor has a finger or two missing as a reminder.

Once the cable is out and you are satisfied it is stretching nicely along the bottom, take the engine out of gear and watch some natural transit abeam of you. There always is one, even if it's only a cow chewing the cud in line with a useful farmer who has knocked off ploughing for a smoke. When the cow and old Giles stop moving in relation to one another, put the engine gently astern once more. The

▶ Boats lying at various angles in the breeze, as these are, indicate that the tide may be unpredictable. Look closely at the one nearest to the mooring you are headed for to see what might happen to your own boat.

transit will start to open until the anchor bites, at which point all relative motion will cease. Now increase the revs to about half speed and really work that hook into the seabed. There will be some initial movement, then, if all is well, you will hang back from the hook and go nowhere. Result: total confidence. Find a new transit to make doubly sure you are not dragging, and that's it. Hoist the black ball from a headsail halyard to show the world you are anchored, or switch on the all-round white anchor light at night, then settle down to enjoy the peace.

A touch of realism

Don't be dismayed when you try anchoring and discover that the boat doesn't want to toddle away astern in a perfect straight line. Her head will probably blow off to one side, perhaps exacerbated by the prop-walk. If this happens, be of good heart, bear in mind what it is you are trying to achieve – cable laid out along the bottom – and that this will very likely happen almost as well if you let her drift, encouraging her with as little power as appropriate.

SKIPPER'S TIP   **THE QUESTION OF TIDE**

Don't forget that in home waters the tide will rise and fall while you are anchored. Refer to your completed tidal height curve (Chapter 12), or your tide computer, and make sure you are embarrassed neither by running out of scope at High Water, nor stranding at Low.

● MANOEUVRES UNDER SAIL

So long as you have a reliable engine, don't over-stress yourself to tackle all these sailing manoeuvres too soon. Managed smoothly, they are really well on towards Coastal Skipper level of competence. Have a go when you're ready, though. Mastering them is the essence of seamanship and can be a source of tremendous satisfaction.

Mooring

Mooring under sail follows the same rules as under power, except that you have no brakes. All you can do is take way off. This is achieved by spilling wind, or letting the sheets off until the sails flap. If they're flapping, they aren't driving, so the boat will slow down and ultimately come more or less to a standstill. Because it is set from the forestay and there are no shrouds to restrict its movement, a headsail can be spilled on any point of sailing. A mainsail, or a ketch's mizzen, can only be spilled, or 'de-powered', when the wind is well forward of the beam (Fig 14.1).

Wind forward of the beam

If the wind is forward of the beam when you are approaching a mooring at the desired angle (ie, the one at which the boat will end up when moored with her sails down), you can control your speed and lose way by spilling the main and the

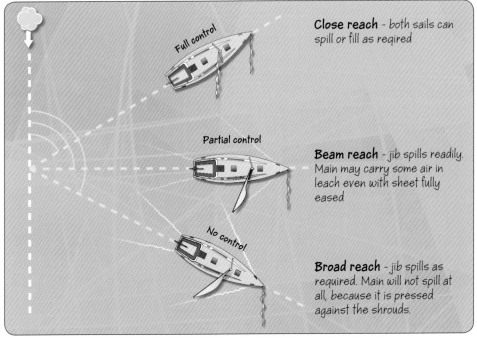

Close reach - both sails can spill or fill as reqired

Full control

Partial control

Beam reach - jib spills readily. Main may carry some air in leach even with sheet fully eased

No control

Broad reach - jib spills as required. Main will not spill at all, because it is pressed against the shrouds.

▶ Fig 14.1 Boat control under sail.

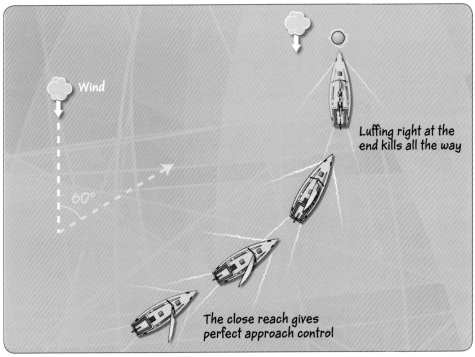

Wind

60°

Luffing right at the end kills all the way

The close reach gives perfect approach control

▶ Fig 14.2 Mooring under sail – no tide or wind with tide.

jib as necessary. It pays to steer for a point a boat's length or so to leeward of the buoy, then come head-to-wind right at the end to luff off* the last of your way. This is the classic manoeuvre with no tide, or when wind and tide are more or less together. If your boat sails adequately under main alone, you might try refining this technique by approaching under main only. There's less to do, and the foredeck crew won't be brained by the genoa clew as they pick up the buoy (Fig 14.2).

Wind against tide

You'll recall that with the wind blowing contrary to the tide, a skipper generally moors upstream when under power. The same applies under sail, because if you try to luff head-to-wind, the tide will be right behind you and will carry you straight past the buoy. Even if you're lucky enough to hook it, chaos will ensue as the tide then swings the boat stern-to-wind and she gybes around the mooring. The only way to pick up a wind-against-tide mooring is to drop the mainsail and approach up-tide under headsail only. You can then spill wind from the genoa easily. Where the windage of the flogging sail is carrying you on past the buoy, roll some up. If even this doesn't get rid of your way, roll the lot in and blow down onto the mooring under bare poles*. After all, it's easy enough to let some headsail out again if you lose control (Fig 14.3).

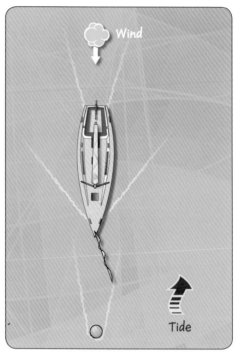

▶ Fig 14.3 Mooring with wind against tide. Drop the mainsail and stow it. Approach the buoy head into tide (downwind) with jib flapping, drawing a little, or even rolled away if the wind demands it. Good control is easy, as long as you let the tide slow you down.

Wind across tide

Often, the wind will be blowing across the tide, rendering the situation ambiguous. If you are unsure, come in under headsail only and remember the old seaman's maxim, 'When in doubt, drop the main!'.

Leaving a mooring

The same rules apply when you are preparing to slip a mooring under sail. Take a look around and ask yourself, 'The way my boat is lying, will the main spill wind if I hoist it on the mooring, easing the sheet if need be?'.

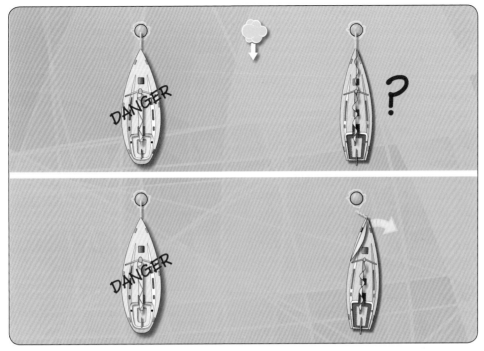

▶ Fig 14.4 Leaving a mooring head-to-wind. To be sure of leaving a mooring on the tack you want, back the jib towards the danger in order to blow the yacht's head away from it.

If the answer is 'Yes,' pull it up. Next, check that the mooring is ready to slip and hoist the jib. To make sure you pay off on the tack you want, pull the jib aback* onto what will be the weather side (to starboard if you intend leaving on the starboard tack). This will blow the head across the wind as you drop the mooring. As soon as you're sure you are on the tack you want, let draw the headsail (send it across to the correct side) and away you go (Fig 14.4).

If the answer to the big question is, 'No, I don't think the main will spill. It will try to fill as I hoist it, even with the sheet right off,' the job is simple. Don't mess with the mainsail. You don't need the drama. Just unroll or hoist some genoa, slip the buoy, sheet in and sail away until you have found some searoom. Now bring the boat onto a close reach, let off the mainsheet and hoist the sail.

Boats with fully battened mainsails find this sort of handling difficult, as in many cases the boat must be dead head-to-wind in order to hoist or lower the sail. This is a distinct drawback, but there are advantages to offset it. If your boat is so equipped, don't expect an easy ride sailing up to moorings or the anchor. Just be grateful for a reliable diesel engine or, if you don't have one, sort it out. For such a yacht, it is very much top of the priorities list.

Anchoring

For anchoring, and weighing anchor under sail, follow the same guidelines as for mooring. The only difference is that because anchoring is less positive and involves a drift while the hook digs in, it sometimes pays to drop all sails as you let the cable go. This is because if the boat's head blows off, as it often does, you may find the main filling even with the sheet fully overhauled when this is the last thing you want. I used to own a yacht whose bow blew downwind as she lost way. After much experiment, I settled for dropping my main at the same time as my anchor and never doubted the practice until one day an old buffer told me it was unseamanlike. I still can't see the sense in his point of view. If things went to the bad, I had only to hoist a headsail (always easy) to regain control, whereas leaving that main hoisted and half-filling left me in awkward straits time and again. So bear the essential principles in mind, do what seems sensible and never mind Captain Blimp.

Digging in an anchor under sail

The best way to ensure this has been achieved is to sail backwards after dropping the anchor. If you want to try it, come head-to-wind and let go the anchor as you lose the last of your way. Now shove the boom out as square as you can get it and steer away astern just as you would under power. When the anchor bites you'll know.

If this seems like too much trouble, lay the anchor under sail, quietly start the engine and give it a tweak astern, lining up old Farmer Giles with Buttercup again to make sure.

Slow speed turns

When we were talking about handling the yacht under power, we established the principle that when turning, she pivots around a central area in her keel. This point is actually called the 'centre of lateral resistance' because if all her power to counteract the tendency of her sails to drive her sideways were concentrated into one spot, this would be it. It follows that at speeds too low for the rudder to bite, any sideways power that can be applied forward of this point will swivel the yacht's bow away from the wind, while anything pushing from abaft it will swivel the stern to leeward. As the stern is forced downwind, the bows pivot upwind, so we can state the following rule:

SKIPPER'S TIP   STEERING WITH SAILS

When the boat is stalled – or almost dead in the water – and side-on to the wind, if the main is pulled and the jib spilled she will luff. If the main is spilled and the jib pulled in hard or backed, she will bear away.

This proposition is the basis of all slow-speed boat handling under sail. Understanding it and practising it beforehand can save the day in all manner of tight situations. Here are one or two of its applications:

- When leaving a mooring surrounded by other boats, it is sometimes necessary to bear away smartly. When you have been lying head-to-wind, this is achieved by overhauling the mainsheet before backing the jib and slipping the mooring. Thus, because the main will flap as the bow falls off the wind, there is nothing to stop the boat turning away until the main starts to fill with the wind abaft the beam. Try the same manoeuvre with the main pinned in tight and you're in for a bad time.

- Approaching a head-to-wind mooring on a close reach, you lose too much way and the yacht's bow blows off. It's no use shoving the tiller to leeward, because the rudder isn't working. It has stalled. That's why the boat is swinging. The only way to regain control is to pull in the mainsheet and get that main drawing positively. As it does, you'll see the bow turn up to windward and feel the rudder begin to grip again.

Sailing alongside

I can't recommend that you do this for fun until you are totally confident of your abilities, and even then you'll find that most of today's harbourmasters take a dim view of it. Sadly, however, the world is less than perfect and you may find you need to try it in an emergency.

However smart her skipper, a boat sailing up to a berth usually doesn't stop perfectly exactly where he would like. It will almost certainly be necessary to take off the last of her way with a judiciously applied rope. Use either a stern line or a spring run from an amidships cleat. Either of these should bring her to a halt without the bow swinging in and the stern careering outwards. Have your most agile crew member step off as you come in, carrying as much rope as required, plus half as much again for good luck. Snatch a turn around a strong-looking dock cleat, then apply steadily more pressure to the rope as it surges round it. Don't just make it up. If the boat is doing two knots, it may well break the line or rip up the cleat. Stopping five tons dead releases a massive amount of energy.

As far as handling the boat is concerned, treat the job as if you were coming up to a mooring and apply the same rules. There's only one extra tip:

SKIPPER'S TIP   THE BAIL-OUT RULE

As with all manoeuvres where obstacles or other boats are in close proximity, never commit yourself until you have worked out an escape route in case things go wrong.

● FURTHER SKILLS

Sail changes at sea

With the advent of roller-reefing headsails, this activity is now only undertaken in a few cruising yachts. If it becomes necessary to change a jib out at sea, do all you can to ease the pain of the poor souls up on the foredeck. Don't just keep on slamming to windward. If you do, they'll be half drowned in no time at all, especially if you are changing down in a rising wind. If you're closehauled, it's a kindness to turn briefly downwind while the hands work their way forward, and keep going in that direction until they have dropped the jib. As soon as she's under main alone, the yacht will slow down enough to let them carry on in comparative peace, allowing you to put the boat back on course.

An alternative solution for keeping the troops dry is to come onto a close reach then ease both main and headsail sheets so that the boat remains under control but is going so slow she is almost stalled. This works well when searoom is at a premium.

Sailing under main alone

From time to time it is convenient to make progress with no headsail set, often as part of a manoeuvre. When sailing close to the wind under main only, ease the sheet a little way and don't try to point too high, however tempted you may be. A main pinned hard in with no jib set develops almost no forward power at all. It is only pulled near to the midships line in order to stop it from lifting when a genoa is set in front of it. As soon as the headsail is rolled away, the main becomes a different sail. Treat it as such and the boat will sail surprisingly well, if a trifle slowly.

Motorsailing

You could be forgiven for thinking I have taken leave of my senses to put motor-sailing into this book and label it a 'skill'. I suppose there are still a few die-hard purists who consider motorsailing somehow poor form, or unsporting. The truth is, however, that for most of us with jobs to go to and schedules to keep, the ability to motorsail realistically in light weather or to windward in a blow has enlarged our cruising horizons and saved many an unpleasant interview with the boss a day after work was supposed to have recommenced. Motorsailing can also enable you to catch a tide or to get home before the lock closes for the night. It is part of modern yachting and should be accepted as such.

Occasionally, I start my engine when I have all sails up and drawing just to speed things up if I'm in a hurry. No special techniques are required here, beyond an awareness that as you gather way, the apparent wind will move forward and you'll be obliged to re-trim your sails. If the breeze is dropping, at some stage the relative airstream from ahead will overcome what true wind remains and you'll find that if you stay on course, you can't sheet your genoa any more. You are now motorsailing into the no-go zone. Roll away the headsail, or drop it and take whatever action you can to flatten your mainsail. Lots of kicker, plenty of halyard tension, and sheet hard in. Traveller should be amidships. Like this, you may well

▶ This yacht appears to be sailing, but is actually motorsailing as can be seen by the black cone in her fore rigging. The collision regulations make it clear that such a shape should be exhibited because otherwise the yacht would appear to have the rights of a vessel under sail; power-driven vessels would be obliged to give way to her.

find you can maintain your desired heading. If the apparent wind comes so far ahead that the main itself starts flapping, you have two choices:

■ When the wind is extremely light, it may prove acceptable to motor straight into it and live with a bit of fuss from the mainsail. You aren't technically motor-sailing now, rather motoring dead into the wind with the main flapping, so you could just take it down. If you do and you're out at sea, the boat may lose some of her ease of motion, because the main has been steadying her as she ploughs through the seas. It's your choice. Either drop it and roll, or leave it up and suffer some annoyance.

■ Motorsailing into a stronger breeze, it is bad practice to let the main flog. Not only does the noise drive a sensitive sailor to distraction, the sail is doing itself no good. In these circumstances, it is better to reef it, flatten it and strap it in tight, then bear away until it just goes to sleep. This will probably be around 25° from the apparent wind, or 35° from the true wind. The additional distance to cover to a destination dead to windward at these angles is surprisingly small, and you will more than make up for it in increased speed and, of course, that oft-forgotten factor of sheer comfort.

The black cone

When motorsailing, all your special rights as a sailing boat under the collision regulations are removed, so other people need to know when you put your engine into gear. Before that, you are still sailing, even if your engine is running. With the propeller turning, you are a motor vessel once again. To remove any ambiguity, the colregs* demand that a motorsailing yacht displays a black cone hoisted point downwards. In practice, to comply with this is distinctly tiresome, particularly as anyone who knows anything about the subject can tell when a boat is motorsailing by looking at her, but display that cone you must if you want to be sure of avoiding prosecution. Fortunately, a collapsible plastic cone costs very little and generally comes as part of a kit along with a similar stowaway anchor ball. I bought my pair at a boat jumble for ten pounds.

Motoring in rivers

It goes without saying that, while it is perfectly acceptable to motor down the centre of a river when you are the only traffic, any approaching vessels must be passed 'port to port'. In plain English, this means you keep to the right. For some reason, helming a boat up a river puts the skipper into the frame of mind of a road vehicle driver. Perhaps it is because a river has banks, but regardless of why it happens it can cause difficulties.

A yacht has no rear-view mirrors, so it is important to keep looking astern. It's surprising how rapidly an overtaking vessel can tiptoe up behind you. When you are being overtaken, do what you can to help the other helmsman, even though it's technically his duty to stay clear. Keep well in to your own side and don't hesitate to take off way in order to shorten the overtaking period. Boat speeds are generally closer to one another than car speeds and two yachts proceeding on parallel courses up a narrow waterway can present an unneccessary hazard.

One final point: my crew always seem to want a closer look at what's coming. Presumably with this in mind, they tend to gang up on the foredeck creating a human wall through which I cannot see. Try to be polite when you tell them to 'siddown'!

15

EMERGENCIES AND HOW TO PREVENT THEM

Eric Hiscock, the pioneering ocean cruiser and author, once remarked to the effect that he worked hard to make his passages as free of fuss as possible. This didn't mean that they were boring. The philosophy he was propounding was that by foreseeing everything that could go wrong, he was generally able to forestall it. This is the essence of seamanship and it's significant that listening in to a conversation between a group of hardened deep-water veterans, you rarely hear yarns of the, 'it was so windy the whole mainsail blew clean out if its bolt-ropes', variety. This chapter is headed, 'Emergencies'. In the second half we'll talk about how to make the most of outside assistance, but the whole effort of seamen should be concentrated on self-reliance, and making sure they never have to call.

● KEEPING OUT OF TROUBLE

Skippering is all about keeping clear of trouble, and you should strive to develop eyes in the back of your oilskin hood that are always on the lookout for it. Here is a sample of the things I am permanently asking myself on passage:

- Has the gas been turned off after the last cup of tea?

- Is the person steering giving enough clearance to that buoy towards which the tide is setting us?

- Do I keep to the windward side of this river I'm sailing up in order to maintain a safe distance from the lee shore? I know it may be technically the wrong one by the colregs, but which is more important on the day?

- The helmsman is steering 'by the lee'*. Do I tell him to wake up, or just remind Aunt Jemima to sit clear of the boom in case we gybe? I don't want her concussed or overboard if the boom comes crashing across.

- I can see one or two yachts a mile or so to windward heeling heavily under that black cloud. Should I take a reef now in good time, or hang on and hope for the best?

- The berth I'm in is handy for the showers and the shops, but it's open to the west. How will it be at midnight if the wind really does go south-westerly as the forecaster hinted, then blow a gale? Perhaps I should accept the inconvenience and the unpopularity with the crew, and moor up somewhere else...

Any or all of these issues can turn a lovely cruise into a nightmare if allowed to develop into problems, and it is all too easy for a single minor mishap handled badly to escalate into a full-blown horror show. Start thinking defensively from the beginning.

Major problems

When things go wrong, they frequently do it in one of a number of definable ways, all of which can generally be forstalled. With the exception of 'man overboard', the main ones are arranged below to remind you to look out for them and nip them in the bud. Losing a crew member over the side is so specific an event that it can be made the subject of a drill. We'll therefore take it on board after the others.

Stranding

This means piling up on a shoal, a beach or the rocks. It happens for three reasons. Either you are not where you thought you were – perhaps the commonest cause – you have lost your engine in windless conditions, or the yacht has come too close to a lee shore in heavy weather for her sails and engine to drive her off.

The answer to the first cause is navigational vigilance. Never force the facts to fit into some preconception of where you might be. If what you are seeing doesn't ring true with your chart, in any way at all, look again and work back to find what's gone wrong. Do not, under any circumstances, reassure yourself in the following manner: 'Oh, I suppose they've moved that buoy for some reason...'

If you are drifting into danger in a calm and have lost your engine, perhaps through the common misfortune of fouling the propeller, by all means call for assistance, but never forget that you have an anchor. Now is the time to use it. Let go as the water shoals and you may well save yourself.

To be driven up a lee shore in heavy weather is one of the classic ways of losing one's ship. Develop a lively respect for all lee shores, and only go near them when you've no choice, especially when it's windy.

Foundering

Sinking at sea in a modern yacht in anything other than the most extreme weather imaginable generally results from failure of an underwater fitting.

Make sure you know your boat's skin fittings intimately, including the stern tube for the propeller shaft. They're all in Chapter 1. Be certain the seacocks are serviced annually and that they all work. Take a look round the boat and make sure there is a set of tapered softwood bungs aboard (buy them ready-made from that amicable chandler) and a hammer to whack them in with if necessary. In addition to this precaution, no boat should go to sea without a selection of stainless steel hose clamps of the 'jubilee clip' type.

Fire

We've been at pains a number of times in this book to make sure that fire or gas explosion never happens, but despite today's regulations for small commercial vessels and generally increased awareness, fire still occasionally takes hold. With the very rare exception of explosion, it remains one of the worst emergencies that can occur aboard for the simple reason that you can't run out of the door and into the street to save yourself.

When fire breaks out, the first priority is to have all hands on deck as sharply as possible. Keep one fire extinguisher near the companionway so you can grab it, then turn round to fight the fire with a safe retreat open behind you. Stowing the hand-held VHF near the companionway is sensible for the same obvious reason. If you can't get back in, you'll be delighted you remembered to pick it up as you exited the hatch.

A second extinguisher is best installed beside the forehatch in case you have to work your way back in from forward. If you have a third, site it in the galley where most fires start.

The engine box should either have a dedicated extinguisher inside, triggered by excess heat, or at least a hole conveniently sited for the firefighter to poke one of the other extinguishers into it and squirt. If you suspect a fire in there, don't open the lid up to look. You'll admit more oxygen and if you're lucky you'll only lose your eyebrows. Apply the extinguisher instead.

A fire blanket by the cooker to smother a small cooking fire is a useful and common precaution.

Collision

A coming together with a large vessel is generally terminal for the yacht. Don't sail too close, remember to wear lifejackets in fog, and don't stand on your rights, always bearing in mind the...

> '...sorry tale of Seaman Day,
> Who perished maintaining his right of way,
> He was right, dead right, as he sailed along,
> But he's just as dead as if he'd been wrong.'

Engine failure

A surprising number of lifeboat call-outs are made by sailing yachts which, for one reason or another, have lost their auxiliary power.

The most common causes of this are detailed under 'Engine Troubleshooting' in Chapter 5. Take this seriously and carry a decent tool kit with carefully selected spare parts, because if the diesel stops or won't start, there really is every chance a well-prepared amateur can fix it.

Should you suffer the misery of a rope or a net around the propeller, there is an outside chance that if you grab it with the boat hook you can unwind it – try putting the gearbox astern (ahead if you were going astern when you fouled your screw), pulling the stop lever to make sure the engine doesn't start, then cranking it with the starter motor. The shaft will turn at a modest speed in the opposite direction to that which wound on the rope. If it's calm enough, not too cold and you're confident you can get back aboard, try diving and cutting the obstruction clear with a breadknife or hacksaw.

When all fails, forget the engine and sail the boat to safety. If in any doubt about tackling the home berth under canvas alone, work into the nearest safe anchorage, let go the hook, launch the dinghy and send for help. People have managed very well without engines from the dawn of time. The first auxiliaries were only fitted into ordinary yachts in the 1930s, and for years many of them were highly unreliable. Nobody thought twice about sailing in, at least to a mooring or anchor, and boats in those days weren't half so handy as ours are.

● MAN OVERBOARD

It might sound like stating the blatantly self-evident, but the best advice I can give about man overboard is, don't let it happen. Even on a nice day, someone going 'over the wall' is a very bad scene indeed. Keep your prudent hat firmly on your head at all times, watch your crew and if they seem more at risk than usual when they aren't clipped on, tell them to be careful. A diplomatic skipper can always make light of this while getting the point firmly across. I often actually tell people to watch out, but I like to hope I do it in a way that doesn't offend.

If you do lose someone, you must act promptly and positively. Man overboard recovery is a three-stage affair: regaining touch, lifting aboard and after-care. Here's the drill for regaining touch in a typical short-handed modern yacht:

1   Shout 'Man overboard!' and crash stop the boat. This means steering through a tack (1a), but not releasing the jib sheet (1b). After the yacht has come through the wind, she will be moving slowly because of the backed jib (1c). You will still be near the casualty and may be able to pass close enough to get a line to him. At this point if not earlier, you must designate an observer if enough crew are on deck. The observer's

job is to point at the casualty continuously until rescue is effected. This task is vital, as losing touch is an ever-present danger. If you haven't enough crew for an observer, do the best you can yourself.

2   If the boat is going too fast as you approach the casualty, or has not come close enough, deploy the man overboard safety gear as you go by. You won't be too far off to throw it. Reassure the casualty and go on to stage 3.

3   Roll away your headsail, or drop the jib.

3a Check all round the boat to make absolutely certain no ropes are in the water.

4   Start the engine.

4a Check a second time for ropes.

5   Motor to leeward of the casualty, gybe, then steer upwind towards him with the mainsail flapping and the breeze slightly on one side of the bow.

6   Stop with the casualty just forward of the lee-side beam. Do not use astern propulsion unless it is absolutely necessary. If you have no choice, be aware of the dreadful possibility of catching feet in the propeller.

7   Pass down a rope and secure the casualty alongside.

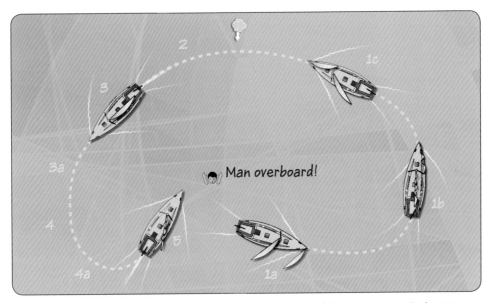

▶ Fig 15.1 Man overboard recovery using sail and engine. Numbers follow stages given in the text.

It's absolutely crucial that you practise bringing the boat back to a person in the water. Even the coolest brains don't function well in times of extreme stress and danger. A well worked-out drill in which you have confidence can save lives if the real thing should happen.

Use a fender tied securely to a bucket as your casualty, but keep the lanyard short otherwise you may steam between the two in the early stages. This is a classic mishap, and you don't need the additional problem of the man overboard exercise dummy round your propeller if you miss.

With the casualty secure, pass smoothly on to Phase two of the operation, that of getting a tired, water-heavy casualty back on board. It's unlikely you'll be able to lift him directly out of the water, and the chances are that unless the boat is low-slung and the casualty is fit, he won't be able to do much to help himself. Various options present themselves:

- If you have a portable ladder, set it up to leeward and help the casualty clamber aboard. In this case, it will help to undo the bottom guard rail, or even both of them. Many yachts secure these with a lanyard so they can quickly be knifed in an emergency.

- Stern bathing ladders offer a seductive solution, but be careful. Lay the boat beam-on to the waves so that she rolls rather than pitches. Rolling, the ladder

▶ A workable set of man overboard safety gear for daylight passages in reasonable weather – a horse-shoe lifebuoy attached to a dan buoy with an extending 'mast' to attract attention. To be fully equipped for all contingencies, the kit would also feature a flashing light and drogue to minimise drift in heavy winds.

will be reasonably stable, but if the yacht is pitching, there is real possibility that it will plunge down and injure the casualty.

- Where neither of these options exist, you must contrive some means of lifting using the yacht's gear. An electric windlass is the best answer. Take a halyard to the windlass warping drum via a snatch block* and attach the other end to the casualty by his harness if he has one on. If not, you'll have to contrive a bowline under his arms, either by his own efforts or some other means unless the boat is equipped, as it should be, with one of the proprietary devices for lifting casualties such as a Tribuckle. Now hit the winch button. Up they come every time, even the rugby forwards.

  No power windlass? Try leading a spare halyard, or even the topping lift, through blocks to a primary sheet winch. These are usually the biggest ones aboard, and you need all the help you can get.

- Some yachts carry a dedicated tackle that is brought out of its locker when required. One block is attached to the casualty, the other to a spare halyard. The tackle is overhauled and hoisted to a convenient height and the hauling end led via any necessary blocks to the winch. Wind away. You definitely aren't going to run out of power this time.

As with the manoeuvre, all this is nothing more than bar-room conversation until you have actually sorted out the gear, practised, and know you can manage should the time ever come. Wait for a sunny day when people are bathing as you lie to anchor and if you aren't completely confident of the boat's ladders, have fun discovering the best way of lifting a heavy victim out. Rig your 'casualty' up in a harness so he won't be hurt by the lift. If no volunteers come forward, lash together a couple of 5-gallon jerry cans, fill them with water and see how you get on with them. It's a salutary experience.

Phase 3, the after-care of an overboard victim, is really a medical matter and you should take the casualty to a doctor as soon as possible, even if he appears hale and hearty. Unless it really was a flat calm summer's afternoon with the swimmer a fit person who laughed as he fell and was still smiling as you recovered him, there is almost always some element of shock. If water has entered the lungs, it is a serious matter and your duty is to seek advice. Until this can be arranged, keep the victim warm and rested. If he is cold, hypothermia is a real hazard, so wrap him in a sleeping bag out of the wind so that the body temperature can slowly recover. Resist the temptation to administer a healing shot from your favourite rum bottle. Save it for after the doctor has been.

Man overboard under sail

In these days of reliable engines, it is unlikely that you will find it neccessary to perform an overboard recovery under sail alone. However, if the engine should fail or, despite your best endeavours, the propeller is fouled, you may be left with no alternative. The most reliable way of returning to a casualty and stopping under sail is to approach as though he were a mooring in a no-tide situation. Tide is irrelevant in overboard manoeuvres because both you and the victim are equally affected by any stream. You must therefore contrive to make the approach on a close reach, losing the last of your way when the casualty is under your lee bow.

■ This is easier said than done, and can only be reliably achieved with a good deal of practice. See Fig 15.2 with text, below.

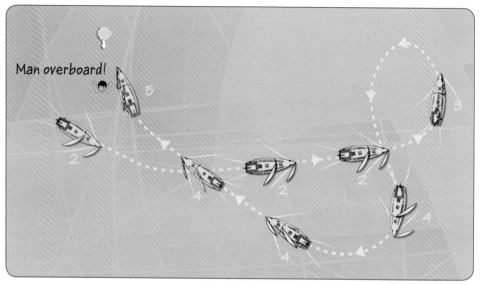

▶ Fig 15.2 Man overboard recovery using sail only. The initial crash stop is the same as shown in Fig. 15.1. This yacht has kept her headsail up so it is available to keep full power on in a seaway. As mentioned in the text, it is often less dramatic to roll away the genoa at stage 2.

1 Crash-stop as before.

2 Try picking up straight away. It may work. If not, deploy safety gear and nominate someone to 'mark' the casualty. Then sail off with the wind abeam to gain searoom.

3 Now tack as tightly as you can, and drop or roll away the jib.

4 Note the position of the casualty, bear away hard and sail downwind until, as you alter course to steer towards him, the boat is close reaching. As soon as you are on course for the casualty, let off the mainsheet and make sure the sail can spill wind. Approach alternatively spilling wind then heaving in the mainsheet to control speed.

5 As the victim comes alongside, luff off the last of your way by steering almost head to wind, just as you would in a mooring pick-up.

The trick is to find that close reach. If you are too far downwind, you will not reach the person and will be obliged to tack up to him. Too far upwind and the main won't spill. Then you can't stop. Often it will be necessary to make more than one positive alteration of course on the same approach run, bearing away or coming up to windward as necessary before trying again.

GENERAL DISTRESS, AND SEARCH AND RESCUE ASSISTANCE

Making a distress call

A distress call can legitimately be made at any time that grave and imminent danger exists to life or the vessel, and immediate assistance is required. This is official wording and means what it says. It does not include a yacht that has run out of diesel on a sunny day with no other difficulties, but it would definitely cover one that was dismasted with a rope round her propeller drifting towards a shoal half a mile away in a gale of wind. Theoretically, a man overboard, unless it is the skipper, is considered a case of urgency rather than distress, but no SAR (Search and Rescue) crew I have spoken with would object if you treated it as full distress and called accordingly. So don't hesitate on that score. The best definition of distress I heard was from a lifeboat coxswain who observed, 'You're in distress when you know you need help and can't manage on your own.'

The law states that you shouldn't be using a two-way radio without an operator's licence, and I recommend that every skipper attends the excellent and reasonably priced one-day course organised by the RYA with an exam at the end. However, you may find yourself in distress before you take the course and not having a licence should not deter you from saving yourself. The same applies if you are left with no alternative than to designate an unlicensed crew member to operate the radio. Fig 15.3 gives an example of a proper distress broadcast. Have a proforma typed up with your own boat's details, then keep it by the radio. Draw it to everyone's attention and make sure all hands can manage it if need be. They will also need to read the GPS position.

You can expect a prompt response to this call. On the sort of trip you'll be making for the time being, this will generally be from a coastguard who may ask for further information. Keep calm and be ready to advise about whether you'll be firing flares, how dire the situation really is etc. If the SAR services are activated you will soon be joined by either a lifeboat or a helicopter. The coastguard will tell you which, and at what point you should start communicating directly with the rescue vehicle.

If you have a VHF equipped with digital selective calling, all you need do is activate the emergency button. You should follow this up with a full Mayday call, but if this proves impossible, you will almost certainly have attracted attention to who you are, where you are, and the fact that you need urgent help.

Distress calls and Man overboard

Some authorities demand that you call for assistance via the VHF (see below for details) as soon as somebody hits the water, regardless of conditions, crew, skill level or anything else. This is because, not to put things too prissily, helicopter and lifeboat crews prefer to be called out then sent back again rather than arrive ten minutes too late and have to pick up a body – especially one that might have been alive had they been scrambled earlier. The decision is yours as skipper, but the search-and-rescue viewpoint is clear. It must, however, be borne in mind that if you are to have a chance of recovering the person yourself (potentially the quickest option), it remains vital not to lose sight of him. If you go below to the radio and are alone on board, this may well happen, because broadcasting a mayday and responding to an answer all takes vital minutes. If you lose him, all you will then be left with is a GPS position to give the SAR people.

Call	**MAYDAY MAYDAY MAYDAY**
	THIS IS YACHT *MASHER MASHER MASHER*
	MAYDAY YACHT *MASHER*
Position	**POSITION 50° 45.15N 0° 02.65E**
	(((or)))
	APPROXIMATELY 1 MILE SOUTH OF DEADMAN'S HEAD
Message	**STRUCK FLOATING OBJECT**
	MAKING WATER FAST
	REQUIRE IMMEDIATE ASSISTANCE
Number on board	**THREE PEOPLE ON BOARD**
	OVER

▶ Fig 15.3 Sample Mayday distress broadcast.

You must make a rapid decision based on a realistic appraisal of your own ability as a sailor, the strength of your crew, the weather and the condition of the casualty. Forethought about this worst-case scenario is vital.

Flares

Any yacht on passage should carry a set of distress flares. For inshore work this should include two or more hand-held red flares plus a pair of orange smokes. Both of these are for pinpointing your position when SAR assistance is within sight. You'll probably see them before they see you, and a red flare or orange smoke signal

SKIPPER'S TIP **GPS MAN OVERBOARD BUTTON**

Many GPS sets offer a 'Man overboard' function, or at least the capacity to create an instant waypoint at your precise position. To activate it, press the button marked MOB, or 'Mark'. This fixes your location at the moment of the incident, then gives the course and distance back to it. A good idea in theory, but bear in mind that in a 2-knot tide, you and the casualty in the water will have drifted ¼ mile away from this position after 8 minutes. This is because both you and the victim are moving down tide together away from the ground GPS position. Nonetheless, if you are making a Mayday call, take the trouble to hit the button. It will form a good starting point for the SAR services if you lose sight of your man.

leaves them in no doubt about where you are and who you are. Save them until they will do some good, don't blast them off prematurely.

If your kit includes rocket parachute flares, these can be used for a general distress statement akin to a visual Mayday. Let one off, wait a couple of minutes for this one to register with observers, then fire your second. It's highly probable that one or both will be seen and reported.

Towing and the lifeboat arrival

If you are rescued by a lifeboat, try to talk to the coxswain as the boat approaches. This helps him in various ways. Make sure your crew are all in lifejackets and ready to abandon ship should they be told to do so. Depending on the circumstances, the coxswain may decide to tow you in. You can help by preparing the boat. A keel-stepped mast will probably be the best attachment point, but a deck-stepped one won't be. Foredeck cleats sometimes come adrift under the extreme forces of a tow, so beef them up by attaching ropes to them, leading them aft to the primary winches and winding them up till they are creaking. This spreads their load and can save the day.

Under tow, the lifeboat will usually put a crewman on board to watch for chafe at the towrope and generally keep an eye on things. If this doesn't happen, be aware that chafe at the bow is the main source of failure. Watch out for it and do what you can to mitigate it with canvas, plastic hose, etc. Once under tow, steer the boat towards the stern of the lifeboat.

Helicopter rescue

An SAR helicopter generally puts a crew member aboard your yacht. Your job is to help him land safely then do as you are told. Here is the usual sequence in the UK. You'll probably be asked to drop sails and motor:

Preparing the boat

- The pilot is on the aircraft's starboard bow so he approaches your port quarter for best vision. Clear the aft deck of anything that could obstruct the crewman's landing, such as aerials, ensign staffs and boom topping lifts.

- Stand by to be briefed on the VHF. If your problem has not disabled the boat, you'll usually be told to motor hard to windward. The helicopter seems to hang off for a long time as the pilot takes stock of the situation. The down-draught from the rotors may be heavy, although often it is less bad than you expect, but be prepared for some massive noise.

- Once you are motoring under the helicopter, maintain course and speed no matter what.

- If the yacht is not under command, it is possible you'll be told to climb into the dinghy or liferaft for pickup, or even to enter the water. Most yacht emergencies, however, are dealt with by hi-line transfer.

Hi-line transfer

Hi-line transfer allows a rescue crew or a stretcher to be lowered reliably to the boat's cockpit without the helicopter remaining overhead for longer than absolutely necessary.

- A light line (the hi-line) is lowered to you. It has a weight on the end and you should grab either this or the line itself. In theory the hi-line should touch the sea to dump static electricity, but this does not always happen.

- When you've caught the line, flake down the slack onto the cockpit sole, but never, under any circumstances, make it fast. If it fouls your gear, a 'weak link' will break. Handle the hi-line yourself, or have a reliable crew member do it.

- The helicopter now stands off again. Keep working the slack on the line.

- Next, the crew or stretcher is lowered. Use the hi-line to guide what's coming down, and be ready for a serious pull.

- If a crew is lowered, he will take charge as soon as he lands in the cockpit.

- The helicopter crew will lift off any casualties, usually one at a time. Ease the hi-line as the lift takes place, and use it to help stabilise the lift.

- If you have not abandoned ship and are still on board after a casualty has been lifted, release the hi-line when you see the helicopter crew signal.

The liferaft

If the yacht is equipped with a liferaft, you must know how to launch it. The main things to remember are first to check that its painter is securely attached to the boat, then to launch it over the lee side and pull the painter out until it reaches the end. This may be ten metres or more. When you feel resistance, jerk the line and expect a bang as the gas canister is activated to self-inflate the raft. Try to board the raft from the yacht, keeping dry if possible and, when the crew is all aboard, use the safety knife located near the entrance to cut yourself clear of the yacht. Make sure you take the hand-held VHF and, if you have one, the hand-held GPS so as to be able to give the position accurately.

More details of liferaft safe practice are to be found in *The Complete Yachtmaster*, but for goodness sake do not hesitate to undertake short daytime passages if you don't have one. As with engines, rafts have only been around a few decades and many of us crossed oceans happily without them. In extremis, you can generally abandon successfully into a rubber dinghy, and if the question of leaving the boat worries you, keep this half-inflated on the coachroof ready for emergencies. The practice will also save trouble when you want to go ashore from an anchorage.

One final word about rafts: the yacht is the safest place to be, even if she is becoming waterlogged. The raft is a last resort when no other way exists to keep you out of the water. In other words, unless the boat is terminally on fire, if you are going to have to climb down into the raft, don't. Only step up into it as the yacht sinks beneath your feet. A raft is hard to spot for rescuers and definitely not a nice place to be. It is a last ditch for survival.

AND BEYOND...

When I was teaching cruising full-time, I used to like Day Skipper courses best of all, watching a group of comparative novices transformed into decision-making sailors within a week. The job satisfaction this brings to instructors is enormous, and no other course returns so much to its participants for the days they invest. To succeed, students must achieve far more than merely ticking off boxes in a syllabus, they must leave firm in the knowledge that, within the limits imposed by experience, they can cope confidently with what the sea will bring. This is all you need to enjoy being in charge of a yacht, which makes working up to Day Skipper level the most important phase of your nautical education.

Beyond Day Skipper lie the grander heights of Yachtmaster, night passages, gales, foreign shores and the magic of sailing distant seas empty of all human existence save your own boat and her people. Whether or not your horizons extend that far, the satisfaction of your future sailing depends on laying sound foundations now. Assess progress made after each passage, learn its lessons, listen critically to the tales of others, look out for trouble without becoming obsessed by it, and expand your boundaries at a comfortable rate. For the time being at least, may your tides run easy and the winds blow over your quarter as you sail the summer seas.

GLOSSARY

A

Aback	A sail sheeted 'aback' is pulled to the windward side of the boat and appears to be inside out. Used like this, a jib can really shove the bow sideways and is a useful manoeuvring tool.
Abaft	Behind.
Abeam	A direction that is at exactly 90° from the fore-and-aft line of the boat.
Athwartships	Running from side-to-side, as opposed to fore-and-aft.

B

Bare poles	To sail 'under bare poles' is to proceed, usually in heavy weather, by blowing downwind with no sail set and the engine off. The number of masts is irrelevant and sloops do not sail 'under bare pole'!
Backed	To back a headsail is to pull its clew to weather, or windward, thus setting it 'inside out'. The practice is used in manoeuvring under sail to push a boat's head to leeward.
Beam	Literally the width of the boat.
Bear away	To turn away from the wind.
Bend	To attach a rope to an object, eg bend on a sheet means to attach the sheet to the sail.
Bight	The middle part of a rope between the load and the cleat, block or belay. An unloaded bight falls into a curve, and so the term has been transported into coastal topography, where a long shallow bay is sometimes referred to as a 'bight'.
Bilge	That part of the boat below the cabin sole, or floorboards, in which water can collect prior to pump-out.
Bitter end	The very end of a rope. Possibly the term grew into use because of the fact that the strongest point on a traditional boat's foredeck is her bitts.
Block	A pulley on board ship is invariably called a block.

Boot top	A line painted around the boat 'between wind and water', right down by the waterline. Not all boats have one of these. If not, the antifouling paint is usually carried up for a few inches to make things look proper and keep the lower topsides clear of marine growth.
Burgee	Small, triangular flag flow at the masthead. It generally signifies membership of a specific yacht club, but sometimes can be a blank or private flag used mainly as a wind indicator.
By the lee	Steering with the wind aft and on the same side of the stern as the mainsail, thus placing the boat in danger of gybing.

C

Cabin trunk	The vertical sides of the 'coach roof'.
Car	A point of attachment, or of fair-leading for a sheet or clew, adjustable in the fore-and-aft plane. Typically found sliding on a metal track on the side deck (genoa sheet fairlead), or the upper surface of the outboard end of the boom (main clew outhaul).
Cleat	A strong fitting for securing ropes, usually shaped like an elongated letter 'T'.
Clew	The aft lower corner of a sail, to which the sheet attaches.
Coach roof	The structure of the cabin top where it stands proud of the deck.
Coaming	The raised portion of decking surrounding a hatch or cockpit.
Cockpit	The 'well' in the deck from which the yacht is steered.
Colregs	The collision regulations.
Companionway	The main entrance to the accommodation, usually found at the forward end of the cockpit.
Cringle	A reinforced eye worked into the luff or leech of a sail to form the new tack or clew on reefing. Each reef has its own set of two cringles.

D

Draught	The measurement of how deeply a boat sits in the water.
Duckboard	The wooden floorboards found on many yachts' cockpit soles.

E

Ensign	The national flag, or 'colours' displayed from aft by all yachts. British vessels never wear the Union Flag, but always the red, blue or, occasionally, white ensign, all of which feature the Union Flag in the upper left-hand corner.

F

Fairlead	A device for leading a sheet or some other line at the correct angle – often onto a winch. Typically, a fairlead takes the form of a sheave in some sort of metal holder.

Fathom	Six feet to you. Or, if you have swallowed so hard on the metric pill that you don't know what a foot looks like, check the end of your leg and multiply by six. If you are concerned about the European thought police, something around 1.8 metres is about it.
Fiddle	An upright guard an inch or two high along a galley or table edge, which prevents items from sliding off when the boat heels.
Frap	(verb) To use a small line to hold an external halyard away from the mast by tying it out to the shrouds. This is done to stop noise and chafe.
Freeboard	The measure of the height of a yacht's deck above the waterline.

G

Gaff	The spar supporting the upper edge of an old-fashioned type of fore-and-aft rigged, four-cornered mainsail. A vessel that uses such a sail is said to be 'gaff-rigged'.
Galley	The kitchen area aboard.
Gooseneck	The universal joint between the boom and the mast.
Guardrails	The arrangement of wires and stanchions* running around a boat for safety purposes.

H

Halyard	A rope used for hoisting a sail. 'Main halyard' for mainsail, etc.
Heads	A quaint and ancient name now used for a sea toilet. Originally the facility was supplied by a hole in the deck right up forward, hence the name.
Heel	The leaning of a boat in response to the wind blowing in her sails.

J

Jammer	A device for stoppering off the bight of a rope under load. Many can also be released under load, but some require the tension of the rope to be taken onto a winch before releasing the tension.

L

Lanyard	A short line permanently attached to an object and used for securing it.
Lee shore	A shore onto which the wind is blowing.
Leech	The trailing edge of a sail.
Leeward	Downwind.
Long keel	A boat is said to have a long keel when the keel is a part of her hull construction running from well forward right aft to a rudder hung from its trailing edge.
Luff	(noun) The leading edge of a sail. (verb) To steer closer to, or directly into the wind.

M

Mean	'Mean', in the context of high or low water, is the figure for an average tide. Thus, Mean High Water Springs, is the height achieved by an average spring.
Mizzen	The after mast of a ketch or yawl, or some square-riggers.

O

Overhaul	To pull a few feet of slack through a tackle before easing it away. The process assists slacking off when the time comes.

P

Painter	The line which secures a dinghy or liferaft from its bow.
Pennant	The line used to heave down the clew cringle of a mainsail when it is reefed.
Piston hanks	Snap-on devices for attaching a sail to a stay.
Port	The left-hand side of the boat looking forward.
Pulpit	The metal framework (usually stainless steel) around the bows which supports the guardrails and protects people working at the forestay.

Q

Quarter	The side of a boat three-quarters of the way aft from the bow. An object sighted 'over the quarter' is around 45° abaft the beam.

R

Reciprocal	A course diametrically opposed to its predecessor, found by adding or subtracting 180° thus, the reciprocal of 090° is 270°, while the reciprocal of 330° becomes 150°.
Reef(ing)	The process of making a sail smaller in stronger winds.
Reeve	To pass the end of a rope or line through a hole or aperture such as an eye, block or fairlead.

S

Sheave	Pronounced 'shiv'. The 'wheel' inside a pulley block or set into a spar to lead a rope or turn its direction of pull.
Sheet	The rope which controls the set of a sail.
Shrouds	Wire rigging which supports the mast athwartships (sideways).
Slack water	The time when the tidal stream is not running – usually at the point of reversal between ebb and flood.
Snatch block	A block that can be opened to admit the bight of a rope, rather than having to feed the end through.

Stanchion	Stainless steel or bronze rod providing support for the guardrails at the deck edge.
Starboard	The right-hand side of the boat looking forward.
Stern	The back, or aft end of a boat. 'Astern' means behind the boat.

T

Tackle	(pronounced 'taykul') An arrangement of pulley blocks and rope used to gain mechanical advantage. Typical application is a mainsheet.
	Ground tackle [pronounced 'tackle'] is the name given to anchors and their associated cables.
Taffrail	The section of toerail which runs athwartships across the stern.
Tender	A generally accepted term meaning a yacht's dinghy.
Toerail	Raised ledge around the outer deck edge. It may be of wood (traditional), aluminium, plastic or some other compound.
Topsides	In English as spoken in Britain, this term means the sides of the boat between the waterline and the deck. In American English, used without a definite or indefinite article, it can also mean, 'on deck' (" 'I'm going topside now, you guys,' announced Luther, clambering up the hatch".)

W

Warp	(noun) Another word for a heavy rope. Sometimes used for shore lines.
	(verb) To move a vessel using only ropes.
Windage	The sum of those parts of a boat other than the sails that catch the wind.
Windex	Trade name that has passed into general usage. A masthead fitting with an windvane arrow and two aft-facing legs that approximately coincide with the closehauled apparent wind angle.

APPENDIX 1: CHECKLIST FOR LEAVING THE BOAT

One of life's nastier events is to be halfway home, only to begin doubting whether or not you turned the gas off on the boat. A written checklist can remove all possibility of such unpleasantness catching you up. Print out a suitable list to your own requirements, then shrink-wrap it and keep it in the chart table. Set out below is one that works for me.

- Ensure that locker doors are open for ventilation.
- Close engine, head, and any other seacocks.
- Batteries off.
- Check bilge.
- Final turn on stern-tube greaser (if fitted).
- Squirt of head cleaner in bowl.
- Rubbish bagged and put in the dinghy or trolley.
- Halyards frapped* as required.
- Ensign, burgee and any house flags lowered and stowed.
- Tiller/wheel lashed amidships.
- Gas off.
- Winch handles stowed below.
- Any 'stealable' on-deck items (man-overboard gear?) stowed below.
- Fenders secured at the right height.
- Warps are secure and tidy.
- Make sure that mooring warps are chafe-free.
- Grab mobile phone, lock up boat and make sure you've got the car keys!

APPENDIX 2:
MEASUREMENTS

With the exception of depths, which are now given in metres on all charts except American ones, I have preferred throughout this book what, to many, are the user-friendly yards, feet and inches of ancient Britain. However, the metric system is creeping up fast, so I append a few simple 'rules of thumb' for conversion. Those wishing for total accuracy may do better to switch on a mathematical calculator and consult their almanacs.

12 inches = 1 foot
3 feet = 1 yard
1 fathom = 6 feet
200 yards = 1 cable
10 cables = 1 nautical mile
1 nautical mile = 1 minute of latitude

1 inch = 2.5 centimetres
1 yard = a bit short of a metre
1 fathom = about 1.8 metres
1 metre = about 3 feet 31/2 inches
1 square metre (sail area measurement) = about 10 square feet

INDEX